THE ULTIMATE GUIDE TO
HOT RODS
& STREET RODS

THE ULTIMATE GUIDE TO
HOT RODS
& STREET RODS

John Carroll & Garry Stuart

CHARTWELL
BOOKS, INC.

This edition published in 2007 by
CHARTWELL BOOKS, INC.
A division of BOOK SALES, INC.
114 Northfield Avenue
Edison, New Jersey 08837
USA

For all editorial enquiries please contact
Regency House Publishing Ltd at

www.regencyhousepublishing.com

ISBN 13: 978-0-7858-2251-6
ISBN 10: 0-7858-2251-8

Printed in China
by Sino Publishing House Ltd.

ACKNOWLEDGEMENTS
The archive pictures in the Introduction, Chapter 1
and Chapter 2 are from the collection of John
Carroll, while Garry Stuart supplied all the other
photographs for this book, for which we thank
them both.

The photographer Garry Stuart would like to
thank the following for their help and
co-operation:-

Herb & Arlene Jurgenson, Pete Chapouris,
Tony Thacker, Jimmy Shine, David Hanson,
John & Jenny Parker, Mike Parti,
Robert & Suzanne Williams, Troy Ladd,
Boyd Coddington, Kennedy Brothers,
Barry White, Marc & Luc Marcel,
Tony Correia, Gene Winfield, Alex Xydias,
Dustin Darrough, The Petersen Museum,
Matt Bargell- www.rodderboy.com,
Thierry Moreau of St Jean d'Angely, France for
film & processing.

CONTENTS

INTRODUCTION

The automobile is not only regarded as having shaped America, its birth and early life can also be seen as a microcosm of the history of the 20th century – often referred to as the American century. There were automobiles in the streets on the fateful day in 1915, when the *Lusitania*, with her hefty quota of American passengers, was torpedoed by the Germans off southern Ireland. This caused such outrage that a climate of opinion was established that would eventually propel America into the First World War. Ford pickups were used to carry goods, that were by now becoming rapidly devalued after the Crash of 1929, while during the Prohibition era of the 1930s, Chevrolets hauled bootleg liquor. In John Steinbeck's *The Grapes of Wrath* of 1939, Tom Joad, in search of a better life after his farm had been repossessed, used a beaten up old jalopy to transport his family west from Oklahoma to California.

Pickup trucks were used in the construction of the Hoover and Grand Coulee dams, as America worked its way out of the Depression, while automobiles were proving their worth in a military role the day the skies above Pearl Harbor filled with Mitsubishi Zeros, and Dodges and Jeeps would later crash ashore on Pacific beaches to deliver a mighty counterpunch. Dodges and GMCs

older generations. Initially, the movement was at grass-roots level, making its history difficult to chronicle. It was part of a casual and unofficial scene in which its participants raced in the streets, ran red lights, evaded the cops and occasionally landed in jail, while thumbing their noses at the status quo. These pioneers and their machines inspired awe in younger kids and fear in their elders. Stripped-down and hopped-up, hot rods began as a southern Californian phenomenon, 80 years ago, and are now to be found on the streets, at the drag strips, and on dried-out lakes. They range from the souped-up Model Ts of the 1920s, through to the Belly Tank Lakesters of the 1940s and '50s and today's Rat Rods and fibreglass repro rods.

What exactly is a hot rod? According to Webster's dictionary, it is 'an automobile rebuilt or modified for high speed and acceleration', which is true enough, but this is not all. California, especially the place where dried-out lakes are located in the south, is generally regarded as the birthplace of hot rods. There, a cult of backyard mechanics, utilizing junkyard parts, created streamlined, no-nonsense racing machines for competition over straight-line courses, laid out here or on nearby desert flats. In those days, nothing but open country lay between the flats and small towns, such as Pasadena, Glendale and Burbank. This is where hot-rodding began; and since few rodders had more than one vehicle, it was essential that, as well as racing

were used to haul GIs across Europe as part of the Allied effort against Nazi Germany, while cars and trucks assumed even more importance in a post-war world that, by now, had greatly changed: now, when delivering tractor parts, the local John Deere dealer probably arrived in one of the new Fords.

OPPOSITE: A well-attended gathering of Ford Model T owners in 1912.

ABOVE: The 1914 Model T Ford Runabout was a two-seater roadster.

RIGHT: By 1918, Ford was producing this Model TT stakebed truck.

In more recent times, the makers of Sci-Fi movies, looking for something that would encapsulate the spirit of 20th-century America, chose to use an old pickup truck, allowing it to drift weightlessly through space for the crew of the Starship USS *Enterprise* to find many generations into the future. This indicates how far the car has worked its way into the American consciousness.

Hot rods are only a part of this culture: they are not 'just cars', they have become American icons. Hot rods have both made legends and become legends themselves, capturing the spotlight in the world of music and the movies. They once represented youth, rebellion and a lust for life not experienced by

LEFT: Henry Ford with the ten-millionth Model T, shown here with one of his earliest cars.

BELOW LEFT: Chrysler made luxury cars such as this Custom Eight roadster during the 1930s.

OPPOSITE: The Ford Model A replaced the Model T. This sport coupé is powered by a 24-hp sidevalve in-line four-cylinder engine.

them, they could be driven to the lakes and to work and back during the week. Most early hot rods were Ford Model T and Model A roadsters, simply because they were cheap, readily-available and lightweight. The normal procedure was to strip off all the non-essential parts, including fenders, running boards, ornaments and windshield, so that maximum aerodynamics and weight reduction could be achieved. Eventually, coupés and sedans joined the hot-rod ranks: often these heavier models underwent drastic surgery to 'chop their tops' to lower and slope or rake their windshields backwards. Large rear tyres were installed to raise the gear ratio for higher speeds, while the standard-size or smaller tyres on the front helped to lower the car and rake it forward to decrease wind resistance. Rows of slots or louvres were punched into the hood, body and rear deck lid to assist engine cooling and to release trapped air. Sometimes, flat aluminium discs were fitted over the wheel hubs as a way of adding further streamlining.

Nowadays, hot rods are older, the unwritten but sacrosanct rule being that only pre-1948 cars should be used. Originally, hot-rodding was the practice of taking an old,

cheap car, removing weight from it, usually by removing the roof, hood, windshield and fenders, lowering it and changing or tuning the engine to produce more power. The term hot rod is generally believed to have derived from 'hotted roadster' – used in the 1950s and '60s as a derogatory way of describing any car that did not fit into the mainstream. In the 1970s, hot-rodders began to clean up their act by using the term 'street rod', at a time when fashion dictated fat wheels and fancy paint to make a car stand out from the crowd. The current fashion is to keep them clean but still noticeable. Those who adhere to the original idea of a cheap, fast and no-frills build, produce what are often called rat rods, and there has been a huge resurgence of interest in this scene in recent years.

Hot- rodders, including Wally Parks, created the National Hot Rod Association (NHRA) to attract racing away from the

LEFT: Rosie the Riveter exhorted Ford workers to produce more during the Second World War.

BELOW: Dodge's production during the Second World War included thousands of the WC-series weapons carriers.

OPPOSITE: Early hot rods were almost exclusively Ford-based, using mixed and matched components from various models.

streets and onto the tracks. The annual California Hot Rod Reunion and National Hot Rod Reunion are held to honour such pioneers, with the Wally Parks NHRA Motorsports Museum going to the very roots of the sport. There are many magazines dedicated to hot rods, such as *Hot Rod*, *Street Rodder*, and *Popular Hot Rodding*. There are also television shows, such as Hot Rod

Garage, Hot Rod TV and Horsepower TV, which suggests that hot rods are an important part of American culture. Tom Wolfe, the author of *Bonfire of the Vanities*, was one of the first to recognize the importance of hot-rodding in the national psyche, bringing it to mainstream attention in *The Kandy-Kolored Tangerine-Flake Streamline Baby* of 1965. This was Wolfe's first book, a collection of essays designed to take a closer look at the American scene of the early 1960s and focusing on the exotic forms of self-expression that were then flourishing across the USA. Wolfe observed the emergence of intriguing art forms and styles of life that had nothing to do with past culture. In the sub-

LEFT: Workers leaving Ford's giant Rouge Plant in Detroit, Michigan, during 1947.

OPPOSITE: Whitewall tyres, hubcaps and chopped-top – this nostalgic three-window coupé screams hot rod.

culture world of the twist, bouffant hairdos, stock-car racing and rock concerts he found what has been described as 'a uniquely American energy and an American aesthetic'. In the title essay, Wolfe eulogizes the flamboyant customized cars that Californian teenagers were designing and constructing with a single-minded and artistic dedication, even though by 1965 the scene had shifted considerably from its roots.

The accepted history is that the classic hot-rod era lasted from 1945 to the time that muscle cars made their appearance in about 1965, reaching its height in the mid-1950s. During this time, there was an ample supply of what hot-rodders call 'vintage tin', cars manufactured prior to 1948 that could be acquired cheaply. Many of these had sound bodies and frames, but had been junked for mechanical reasons. The classic era of hot-rod construction ended around 1965, not because the supply of vintage tin had dried-up, but because new, factory stock cars now came equipped for greater speed and power, and little, if any, modification was required. By now, the typical hot rod was heavily modified, particularly by replacing the engine and transmission and possibly other components, including the brakes and steering. Certain engines, such as the flathead Ford V8 and the small-block Chevrolet V8,

LEFT: The half-ton Ford F-1 pickup of 1948 was one of Ford's first all-new post-war designs.

OPPOSITE: The heavy-duty Dodge Power Wagon pickup was closely related to the wartime WC models.

magazine, founded by the artist Robert Williams, has thrived in recent years as the latest and greatest extrapolation of kustom kulture art.

While the hot rod has its origins in late-1930s California, when enthusiasts first began to strip down cars – mostly 1932 V8 Fords – so that they could race them, the multi-million dollar sport of drag racing would ultimately be spawned. Meanwhile, hot rods soon began to spread far beyond California, with the result that other types besides Ford cars and roadster pickup trucks were soon rodded; big V8s were installed, roofs were lowered or 'chopped', suspensions were lowered and a host of other modifications were made, limited only by the builder's imagination. The hot-rod truck was a natural progression from the hot-rod car, simply because so many of the light trucks shared the front-end sheetmetal with cars of the same year, and favourites soon included 1930s Ford and Willys models. Pickups had the added attraction of being able to haul all manner of things and be used as back-up trucks, carrying spares and tool kits, for race cars. Ford flathead V8 engines became the power plants of choice after their introduction in 1932. Mass-produced by the million, they were cheap and plentiful, and their design permitted relatively easy performance enhancements. Developing 85hp in stock

were particularly sought after, because of their compact size, ready availability and power. Construction of a hot rod required skill in mechanical work, welding, paint and bodywork.

There is currently a vibrant hot-rod culture in North America, especially on the West Coast. Builders of hot rods, such as Jesse James, also famous for chopping motorcycles, have established themselves as

part of popular culture as a result of TV shows. The Discovery Channel currently transmits modern interpretations of 'kustom kulture', such as Monster Garage, American Hot Rod, and Overhaulin', while *Juxtapoz*

configuration, the earliest modifications usually consisted of removing the muffler, straightening the exhaust pipes and adding multiple carburettors. The results could more than double the original output, producing an engine that could often propel a roadster at over 100mph (160km/h).

By this time, names like Benito Mussolini and Adolf Hitler were increasingly on people's lips. In America, for some at least, the Depression had begun to bottom out by 1933, though many of the farmers of Oklahoma's dustbowl had begun to head west for California and what was perceived as a better life. Photographs of the period show overloaded cars and trucks, laden with poverty-stricken people and their meagre belongings, in scenes reminiscent of fleeing wartime refugees. It was no easy matter to buy cars, trucks or motorcycles in the early 1930s, and the fact that this migration was motorized illustrates the early and widespread significance of the automobile in US society.

The onset of the Second World War brought to an end only the first chapter of the hot-rod story, rather than the scene itself. On joining up, Californians left their dry-lake roadsters and chopped coupés behind in garages or in the 'care' of younger brothers. They took pictures of their cars with them to war, telling tales of their adventures to young men like themselves, who came from every

national menace, by fostering civic-mindedness and co-operation between hot-rodders and the police, and by creating organized drag strips to replace street racing. As a result, many enthusiasts turned to building cars exclusively for drag racing, while others continued to build hot rods, hopped-up cars that could be raced from stop light to stop light, but which in reality were merely stylish transport.

Others began a new trend by modifying cars for looks rather than performance, soon to be known as customs or 'kustoms'. Like early hot rods, they evolved from lower-priced production automobiles, such as Fords, Chevrolets and Mercurys, but unlike hot rods they were in the main more recent models, so rarely came from junkyards. This type of customizing involved severe top-chopping, lowering or channelling the entire frame to within inches of the ground. Seams were filled to smooth the car's lines, and streamlined fender panels, known as skirts, were added to cover the rear wheel-arches. Chromed parts were favoured, as were spare wheel covers (known as continental kits), side-mounted exhaust pipes (called 'lakers' or 'lakes pipes'), and no expense was spared on the custom paintwork. Lights were recessed or 'frenched'

corner of the USA. Consequently, when the war ended in 1945, hot-rodding exploded into the public consciousness, becoming the strongest automotive fad in post-war America. In California, and across the rest of the country, a dangerous, often fatal craze for street racing caught the imagination, and hot-rodders would gather together at local hangouts, cruising up and down at night to show off their cars. Their activities attracted public attention, which focused on what was

perceived as the growing social problem of juvenile delinquency. Along with rock and roll, hot rods were soon identified with the darker side of the American dream, which inevitably made them more popular than before.

In an effort to reverse this negative image, the first Hot Rod Exhibition was held in January 1948, at the National Guard Armoury in Los Angeles. Emphasizing the positive aspects of craftsmanship, engineering and

safety, the show was attended by 10,000 people. Two years later, Robert E Petersen's newly-published *Hot Rod* magazine, the first issues of which were sold at the entrance to the exhibition, boosted the circulation to 300,000. Enthusiast magazines and organizations such as the Southern California Timing Association (SCTA), founded in 1938, and the National Hot Rod Association (NHRA), founded in 1951, were gradually able to change perceptions of hot-rodding as a

into the bodywork, and details such as pinstripes, scallops and flames were added as the era progressed.

The 1960s saw the arrival of the factory 'muscle cars', Detroit's response to performance hot rods. These took the form of plain-looking automobiles, stuffed with huge-displacement engines like the Chevy 396, 409 and 427; the Ford 390 and 427; and the Chrysler 440 and 426 Hemi, so-called for its racing-engineered hemispherical combustion chambers. Advertisements emphasized how ideal a proving ground the drag strip was for the performance engine, which spawned another scene with trends of its own. Trends exist within the hot-rod scene as much as anywhere else, and as hot rods became street rods, so too did the rodded trucks. The fashion for resto rods – a street rod that at a glance appeared to be a restored stock car of the 1970s – suited vintage trucks as well as cars. Meanwhile, alongside the resto rod, the 1932 Ford and 1941 Willys trucks, another trend was beginning to

emerge in the early 1970s, when some began to favour later-model trucks, both pickups and vans. These people wanted to customize or 'rod' them or simply make them better in a particular way, be it for off-roading, drag racing or whatever was required. Vans were treated to bold paint jobs covering large expanses of sheetmetal, and there were wild custom interiors. Classic pickups, such as the 1955 Chevrolets, were lowered, fitted with bigger V8s and painted bright colours. Unlike the street-rod scene, where it had to be a pre-1948 vehicle to be a real rod, the scene welcomed all comers, be they new Japanese compacts or full-sized classics. Mini-trucks soon became a popular sub-section of the scene, simply because they were affordable and plentiful and popular paint jobs included both modern graphics and classic flames.

Street-rod techniques of the 1970s, such as installing a Jaguar IRS (independent rear suspension) in a truck, grew popular in conjunction with engine swaps. By 1977 three main strands had emerged, vanning, classic trucking and modern trucking. The use of flames as decoration became ever more

OPPOSITE: By the 1960s, drag-race machines had evolved a long way from hot rods. This is noted racer, Connie Kalitta's Ford-sponsored 'Bounty Hunter'.

LEFT: Ford built the GT40 to compete in races with European sports cars. It was powered by a hot version of Ford's water-cooled 289-ci (4736-cc) V8. It produced 390hp at 7000rpm.

LEFT: The GT40 brought Ford a 1-2-3 win at the noted Le Mans 24-hour race in 1966 and variations of the model won again in 1968 and 1969.

OPPOSITE: A dressed-up V8 engine, whitewalls, dropped-beam axle and a tall gear-shifter were de rigueur for hot rods of the same era.

pervasive, while the massive murals were reserved for the sides of vans such as Ford's Econoline. Roof chops were another street-rod and custom-car technique that was soon applied to both vans and trucks, and massive gatherings of classic Ford F-100 owners, such as the Reno F-100 run, began to be staged. The off-road and 4x4 scene got bigger still towards the end of the 1970s and increased interest in desert racing introduced a new style to the truck scene, the off-road look. This included the fitting of off-road tyres, pre-runner fenders, lift kits and more.

Another trend emanating from southern California was spawned by the Chicano culture, which refined customizing techniques to produce lowriders, which initially were mostly based on 1963 and 1964 Chevrolet Impalas. These lowriders often emerged as stunning show cars, sporting candy-apple paint jobs, air-brushed murals, crushed-velvet upholstery, and whitewall tyres mounted on deep-dish chrome or gold-plated wire wheel rims. The name of these cars was derived from the components that made them unique, such as hydraulic suspensions that could lift and

heavily-modified. The mini-truck scene began to grow more sophisticated as cabriolet and similar conversions became commonplace, and also began to feature European sports-car styling and components. On the other hand, four-wheel-drive trucks were often fitted with suspension lift kits and with massive off-road tyres on custom wheels to boost their performance in muddy conditions and allow them to scale larger obstacles off-road. Linked to this, the mid-1980s also saw the emergence of the monster show truck; off-roaders on massive wheels and tyres, with a multiple shock absorber set-up and wild finishes. By the mid 1980s the different types of truck were becoming known by specific names: early trucks were known as 'haulers'; fast early trucks remained 'truck rods'; compacts (either US-made or imported) were simply referred to as 'minis'; and late-model custom half-tons became known as 'sport trucks'.

As the 1980s progressed, new events such as truck racing on racetracks became popular and, like desert racing, attracted sponsorship from truck and component manufacturers, while the 1990s saw the mini-trucking and classic scenes boom and diverge to some degree. Meanwhile, the classic scene remained focused on the traditional, while the minis continued to get wilder, with ever-larger stereo systems and more flamboyant and graphic paint jobs. The pro-street, drag-strip look proved popular for trucks. Classic haulers also continued to be popular and there was a new twist, when some began to build street-

lower the car or rake it forward and back, making it hop under the careful control of the driver. Lowriders are still the exclusive province of Chicano customizers operating within strict, trend-led parameters. These lean towards excess and have been known to include dashboards set with integral fish tanks.

By the 1980s the hot-rodding scene had changed, some would say declined, although the flame had not gone out completely. Those with nostalgic feelings for the past had two car clubs, the Los Angeles Roadsters and the Bay Area Roadsters, who began a tradition of long-distance cruising on the state's highways, on rods which by now were largely stylized reworkings of the 1920s and '30s open-top roadsters. These cruises, which had begun in the 1970s, were popularized in car magazines as 'rod runs', and soon spread to other states, assuming the trappings of large-scale family picnics, with show-car competitions and swap meets. The 1980s also saw a resurgence of interest in custom vans and mushrooming interest in vintage and classic trucks, whether they be stock or

OPPOSITE: The Fad T was a 1970s style that caricatured the original Model T Ford, having vintage lights and windshield and a modern engine.

RIGHT: Larry Sterkel's classy, Porsche-red, closed-cab 1935 Ford pickup exudes style, with its billet wheels and attention to detail.

rod haulers from old cab-over-engine trucks on modern chassis. The racetrack series of truck racing became a NASCAR series and attracted top drivers to the multi-round NASCAR championship at venues that included Watkins Glen, Indianapolis, Sears Point and Phoenix International Raceway.

Some of the most spectacular events are the off-road races: in North America, there is a series of desert races run under the auspices of SCORE (Southern California Off Road Enterprises) and HDRA (High Desert Racing Association), of which the two most famous are the Mint 400 and the Baja 1000: these events attracted the interest of established drag-racers and hot-rodders, including Wally Parks and Mickey Thompson. The numerical suffix is an indication of the races' length in miles, while the name is relevant to their locations. The Baja 1000 runs on the Baja California peninsula, Mexico, while the Mint 400 is based in Las Vegas, the Mint being a casino that was once a major sponsor; however, the race is now called the Nissan 400, due to a change in sponsorship. The Baja 1000 has been running for more than 25 years and is regarded as a tough race, as is the Nissan 400. Other American desert races include the Fireworks 250, the Las Vegas 250

and the Parker 400. There are fiercely-contested classes for almost every type of pickup truck, 4x4 and off-road buggy. Some classes attract huge professional teams, sponsored by manufacturers and importers of

4x4s; this is because successful results lead to increased showroom sales.

In recent years, Ford, Chevrolet and Toyota have made strong showings in the truck classes, while Jeep Cherokee racers have

gained honours in the Pro/Stock mini-truck class. Other extensive sponsorship comes from parts and accessory manufacturers, such as tyre companies, and includes BF Goodrich and Yokohama, who regard off-road racing as

an ideal test bed for their products; this also applies to manufacturers of shock absorbers as well as oil companies. These are united under the banner of the Specialty Equipment Manufacturers Association (SEMA), whose showcase event, the SEMA Show, is held annually in Las Vegas. The National Hot Rod Association (NHRA) has turned drag racing into a nationwide spectator sport that is now a worldwide phenomenon.

Hot-Rod Culture

There has long been a place for hot rods in music: Arkie Shibley and the Mountain Dew Boys recorded the first version of George Wilson's *Hot Rod Race* in late 1950. It was one of at least seven recordings of the song, released during the early 1960s and appearing in the country charts. It became one of a sequential series of songs that continues the story of three hot-rodders, street racing in a Ford, a Lincoln and a Model A:

But we had a good race'n' I'll remember the day that me and that Mercury went out to play,
an' there's one more thing I'd like to say, don't try to beat a kid in a hopped-up Model A.

By the time the fifth song in the series came out, it was written from the point of view of the third driver, the kid in the Model A:

If ya ever get mad at a hot-rod kid, remember the things that once you did, when you were young, carefree and gay, and had a hopped-up Model A.

Hot-Rod Lincoln, by Charlie Ryan & the Livingston Brothers, written by Charlie Ryan and released in 1955, is one of the most

LEFT: A 1990s rod-run, hosted by the Goodguys in Dallas, Texas.

OPPOSITE: A late-1990s treatment of a mid-1950s Ford F-100 panel van. Among other changes, the body has been smoothed out and lowered.

famous. Ryan, who owned a real hot-rod Lincoln with a Model A body, began his road race in Lewiston, Idaho, going through to the top of the hill where Chuck Berry would later catch Maybellene in her Coupé de Ville.

Well you've heard the story of the hot-rod race that fatal day,
when the Ford and the Mercury went out to play.
This is the inside story I'm here to say, I was the kid that was a-drivin' that Model A.

Inevitably it ends like a lot of street racing did at the time:

Well, they arrested me, and put me in jail.
I called my pop to go my bail.
He said 'Son, you're gonna drive me to drinkin'
if you don't stop drivin' that hot rod Lincoln.'

Dorsey Lewis' *Hot Rod Boogie*, was released in the mid-1950s. It's about a guy putting a car together piece-by-piece.

Now, the cab and chassis of a Model A, and the springs and shackles of a Chevrolet.
A Mercury motor and a Dodge rear end, and the fenders off an old Terraplane.
Fuel pump off a GMC and the windshield off an ol' Model T.

Commander Cody & The Lost Planet Airmen
and *Asleep at the Wheel* both covered *Hot-
Rod Lincoln*, while Charlie Ryan released two
albums of hot-rod songs around the peak of
his popularity. *Hot Rod* of 1961 was described
in the liner notes as follows: 'This album has
a 3/4 cam, two four-barrel carbs, a hot ignition,
a 270 block, 456 rear end and twin straight
stacks. That's about as souped up as you can
get.'

The Beach Boys immortalized a particular
hot rod – the 1932 Ford coupé – in their
October 1963 hit, *Little Deuce Coupé*, by
Brian Wilson and Roger Christian.

*Well I'm not braggin' babe, so don't put me
down,*
*But I've got the fastest set of wheels in
town,*
*When something comes up to me he don't
even try,*

*'Cause if I had a set of wings, man, I know
she could fly.*
She's my little Deuce coupé
You don't know what I got...

In another style, Bruce Springsteen also
recognized the iconic importance of the Deuce
coupé in the song *Ramrod*, on his 1980
Columbia Records album, *The River*.

*I've been working all week, I'm up to my
neck in hock,*

Come Saturday night I let my Ramrod rock,
*She's a hot-stepping Hemi with a four on
the floor,*
She's a roadrunner engine in a '32 Ford.

Add to these hot-rod movies, such as
American Graffiti, and it's clear that the hot
rod and all the other trends it spawned have
been enormously influential in American
popular culture, especially when one
considers its humble origins.

CHAPTER ONE
THE TEENS & TWENTIES:
THE RISE OF THE INTERNAL COMBUSTION ENGINE

The automobile is so inextricably a part of America's history, that it is no surprise that the hot rod should be a facet of American culture. Just as surely as the horse and the shovel did their bit to shape America, so the automobile was seminal in developing both the land and the nation.

'About you. Tell me about you – what part of Texas are you from?'

'All of it. Wherever my pa could find work.'

'What did he do?'

'Wrangled cattle, and rode rodeo.'

'Sounds fun.'

Jake shrugged. 'I preferred machines to horses.'

'Then?'

'There was this war, and they needed mechanics to drive tanks.'

Cry Wolf, Wilbur Smith (1976)

As suggested above, the history of the automobile began when the transition was made from the horse to the internal combustion engine as the prime source of motive power. What furthered its progress, at the expense of steam and electricity as the primary source of power for vehicles, happened in Texas on 10 January 1901. This was when the huge Spindletop oilfield began producing crude oil for the first time, and it

was from this black gold that kerosene, paraffin, naphtha and later, and crucially, gasoline, was obtained.

The early history of the automobile is inextricably entwined with that of the earliest pickup trucks. Just as there had been horse-drawn vehicles for carrying people, so were there others for transporting goods; later, engine-driven vehicles would follow this pattern, still keeping these separate functions in mind.

Nothing written on the subject of hot rods would be anywhere near complete which omitted the name of Henry Ford and the significance of his influence on the early automobile industry. Ford was born in 1863 near Dearborn, Michigan, on a farm belonging to his father, William Ford. Consequently, Henry grew to manhood with an intimate knowledge of farmwork and the back-breaking drudgery it entailed. This led him to think there might be a better way, and fuelled his interest in mechanical things, at a time when the horse was the only source of power. By 1893 Henry Ford was an employee of the Edison Illuminating Company in Detroit, Michigan, but in his spare time he was experimenting with internal combustion engines, and their potential use in vehicles. Ultimately, he drove his first four-wheeled vehicle, a twin-

cylinder, four-stroke-engined, gasoline-fuelled quadricycle on 4 June 1896. It had two forward gears and was capable of 10mph (16km/h) in low gear and 20mph in high. Then this former farmhand and talented mechanic went on to build another car, while still working at Edison's. This was the auto buggy, a tiller-steered two-cylinder car with a planetary gear transmission and chain drive.

In 1899 Ford left the Edison Illuminating Company and founded the Detroit Auto Company, which at first was heavily involved in car-racing. It later evolved into the Henry Ford Company, which Ford himself eventually abandoned after a disagreement as to the direction the company should take. His intention had been to build low-priced machines for the ordinary man in

only from converted cars. In 1907 the Ford Motor Company built the prototype of what it hoped would be the world's first mass-produced agricultural tractor, and the Model T Delivery Car was introduced in 1912, followed by the Model TT or Model T Ton, a truck with a capacity of one ton. The company also manufactured a range of Model T Roadster pickups and some vehicles specifically constructed as panel vans. At the same time, Henry Ford was experimenting with the moving assembly line, reputedly inspired by the overhead trolley system used in beef-packing factories. This proved a great success and by 1913, 1,000 Model Ts were rolling off the line every day.

There were four large automobile shows

OPPOSITE: Henry Ford in the front passenger seat of the 15-millionth Ford car.

LEFT: The 20-millionth Ford, a Model A, coming off the Ford assembly line.

BELOW: Hupmobiles were made by the Hupp Motor Company of Detroit, founded in 1908. This is a Hupmobile dealership of the 1920s.

in the USA as early as 1900, held in Bedford, Connecticut, Chicago, Illinois, Trenton, New Jersey and at New York's Madison Square Garden. The latter event was by far the largest, and featured 300 vehicles from around 40 manufacturers, run under the

the street, but his colleagues favoured luxury motorcars that would be rather more expensive to produce. Once Ford had left, the company was reorganized, becoming the Cadillac Company. In 1902 Ford built an experimental people's car and in June 1903 he was one of the 13 men who founded the Ford Motor Company, on raised capital of $100,000.

At that time, it is estimated to have cost $25,000 to develop Ford's experimental but affordable Model A, but in the first few months, sales of the Model A exceeded this amount. In 1905 the American Society of Automobile (later Automotive) Engineers (SAE) was formed, and Henry Ford was one

of its vice-presidents. This was at a time when the proponents of steam and electric cars were beginning to fall by the wayside and the internal combustion engine was assuming more and more importance. In the 1906–07 sales year, Ford became the world's largest automaker, producing 8,423 15-hp four-cylinder Model N cars that retailed at $550 each. Ford owned 51 per cent of the company's stock and made a profit of $1 million.

Ford had offered what was described as the Delivery Car in 1905 – basically a Model C automobile with a delivery-type body. It was discontinued in 1906 and between that time and 1911, Ford trucks were constructed

LEFT: A 1920s gas station: development of these was fundamental to the growth of motoring.

OPPOSITE: Ford offered cheap automobiles aimed at a mass market, unlike Lincoln, that concentrated on expensive machines for the few.

auspices of the Auto Club of America, the now better-known Automobile Association of America having been founded in 1902. Oldsmobile is acknowledged to have built the first factory specifically designed for motor-vehicle production in 1901, simply because it had been necessary to rebuild its factory following a disastrous fire, which all but destroyed the business. In the wake of the fire, and in order to resume production, Oldsmobile began to sub-contract other companies to produce the numerous components needed in the production of its cars, a practice that has become widespread throughout the auto industry today. At this time, the US population numbered approximately 76 million, the majority living in rural locations. Roads did exist, but only 150,000 miles (250000km) or so could be described as 'improved': this did not necessarily mean surfaced, as only a mere 150 miles or so could actually be described as such.

At that time, many of the companies that were destined to flourish in the early years of the automobile industry, were already making related items, such as agricultural machines. The International Harvester Corporation (IHC) had its beginnings in the McCormick Reaper of 1831, that

33598-11-9-22
33590

vehicle of its own, the three-quarter-ton Model Three Delivery Car. This was available in two forms, a panel or an express delivery van and a pickup, powered by an in-line four-cylinder engine of 192.4-ci (3153-cc) displacement. It achieved this through a bore and stroke of 3.5 x 5in (89 x 127mm) and produced 30hp. The vehicles remained in production for several years until, in 1918, Studebaker ended all production of its commercial vehicles.

The now-massive GMC started in an equally small way; in 1903, William C Durant took control of Buick and in 1908 founded the General Motors Company, which absorbed a number of other early car- and truck-makers. Starting in 1911, the same year that GM shares were listed on the New York Stock Exchange for the first time, the company's trucks were sold as GMC models, by which time, developments were coming fast and thick. In 1910, the US auto industry produced 187,000 vehicles, around 6,000 of which were trucks and buses, while at the New York auto show that year, the White Steamer company displayed its first gasoline-engined truck: at the same time, Diamond T completely abandoned car production to concentrate on large trucks.

The official line is that the Ford Motor Company has been making a variety of pickup trucks, more usually referred to simply as 'trucks', since 1917, which is the time that Ford began mass-producing them. This coincided with the massive demand for trucks following America's involvement in the First World War. The main supply of trucks prior to this date had come from

subsequently led to the formation of IHC in 1902. By 1907, commercial vehicles were going into production, together with vehicles such as the Auto-Wagon, which offered a choice of panel-van and grain-box bodies. Through the remainder of the decade, the company went on to produce a range of light trucks, including utility wagons and panel vans, but gradually shifted its emphasis to light trucks. A new line of conventional

trucks was introduced in 1915, with payloads ranging upwards from three-quarters of a ton.

Studebaker initially manufactured horse-drawn commercial vehicles in South Bend, Indiana, having been founded in 1852. Henry and Clem Studebaker had a blacksmith's shop in South Bend, where they made wagons for local farmers, but from these humble beginnings noted horse-drawn vehicles evolved, and by 1876 the company

had become a large concern. After experimenting with some early automobile designs, and even electric propulsion around the turn of the century, Studebaker finally introduced an internal combustion-engined automobile in 1902, and subsequently co-operated with other fledgling manufacturers, including the EMF Co and Flanders. By 1914 the company was sufficiently established to introduce a light commercial

smaller companies, which would fabricate a commercial body on a rolling chassis-cab, something Ford produced precisely for this purpose. By 1917 the number of small companies custom-building truck bodies onto Ford chassis-cabs had multiplied, though not all of the work was good. Ford, no doubt correctly, felt that this was likely to reflect badly on his products, so on 27 July 1917, the Ford Motor Company announced a one-ton chassis that would form the basis of the company's own truck programme. This new chassis was stronger than those used on Ford cars and had a wheelbase that was 2ft (0.6m) longer, and had heavier rear suspension and solid tyres on heavy-duty wheels. It was referred to as the Model TT after the car from which it had derived.

By the time the First World War was underway, motor-vehicle production was locked into the American national economy for all time, having by then produced an estimated $700 million worth of vehicles. The wider economic climate also favoured the development of the automobile at this time, with the Federal Aid Road Act encouraging the establishment of highway departments, and offering individual states the financial means to create better roads.

The Dodge brothers began to make automobiles in 1914, becoming seriously involved in the manufacture of commercial variants during the First World War. During America's conflict with Mexico in 1915, a motorized raid on the rebel forces of Pancho Villa was led by George S Patton Junior. He was then a lieutenant and a man who would be famous in later campaigns. Patton's

commanding officer at the time, General 'Black Jack' Pershing, was so taken with the 250 Dodge cars that had been used in the raid, that he insisted Dodges be used in future, as a result of which, Dodge began to build a variety of commercial vehicles for use as troop-carriers, ambulances and light trucks. What was significant was that it was the first time that the US Army had used motor vehicles in battle, at a time when mobility was the province of the cavalry, and army tactics were still based on those of the American Civil and Indian Wars or earlier.

On 6 April 1917, the United States declared war on Germany, despite the fact that its military was not totally prepared. The Democrat president, Thomas Woodrow Wilson, subsequently made a plea to industry, requesting all-out production, and by the time of the Armistice in 1918 a huge number of vehicles had been supplied to the US Army. Dodge's first civilian truck was a civilianized version of the screen-sided panel type, built for the US Army; it also went on sale in 1917.

During the post-war years, other developments affecting the automobile ensued; in 1919 Oregon was the first state to introduce a gasoline tax, when a cent was added to the price of every gallon sold. In the same year, Washington state allocated $65 million to road construction, and around three million miles of roadway eventually stretched across America.

The unpopular 18th Amendment to the US Constitution, which prevented the sale and production of alcohol, had been introduced in January 1920, beginning what is known as the era of Prohibition, which did not end until

1933. By then, the automobile industry was the largest in the USA. The American road network continued to develop: roads oriented north to south were given odd number, while those going east to west had even numbers. On 4 March 1921, Warren G Harding was the first US president to travel to his inauguration by car, on that occasion using a Packard.

That same year, Dodge, together with various other manufacturers, were beginning to look for innovative ways to increase sales in a booming yet fickle market: Dodge, for example, came to an agreement with the Graham company in which it would market Graham trucks (which used Dodge components) through Dodge dealers. By 1923 these trucks had evolved into Dodge passenger cars with Graham commercial bodies – an arrangement that endured until 1928. Change was afoot, however, when Walter P Chrysler acquired Dodge in June 1928. He changed the name of the trucks back to Dodge and fitted them with a four-cylinder Plymouth engine. Production of these machines continued until 1933.

The General Motors Corporation had begun to produce light trucks in the second decade of the 20th century and had produced a range of trucks prior to the First World War. Its early models gained a reputation for both ruggedness and reliability: the Model 16 One-Tonner became the basis for many US Army ambulances during the war, and was the basis of the GMC K-series after the war. GMC acquired Chevrolet during the First World War, following a period when it secretly acquired GM stock. Another merger followed in 1925, to be followed by yet another in

OPPOSITE: The pickup truck was born of necessity as this photograph of James Cargo's 1920s Model T roadster pickup suggests.

1943, with the company increasing in size each time. The first pickups from Chevrolet came in 1918, when the company produced less than 1,000 in both half- and one-ton capacities. The pickups, however, were a success, and in excess of 8,000 were made the following year. In the early 1920s the company installed a variety of outsourced bodies on its chassis-cab trucks, producing them in Chevrolet plants. In 1922, for example, a Chevrolet three-quarter-ton Model G chassis and cowl retailed at $650. This pattern continued through the 1920s, with occasional additions to the range, such as an all-steel enclosed cab model in 1925, as well as a Panel Truck in the same year.

A new line of IHC trucks was introduced in 1921, known as the S-series. The 'S' prefix denoted a 'speed truck', and they were capable of 30mph (48km/h). The range soon acquired the nickname 'Red Babies', due to their diminutive size and red paintwork. The trucks were sold through 170 IHC farm-equipment dealers, who referred to them as 'cornbinders'.

Six Dollars a Day
Sales took a turn for the worse in 1921 as part of an overall economic decline. Henry Ford survived by dropping the price of the Model T to such an extent that 55 per cent of cars sold in that year were Model Ts. He also changed the face of industrial relations by guaranteeing

his employees a five-day working week and $6 per day wages. In 1925 Ford produced the Model T with a pickup body, while other improvements around this time included improved lubrication systems, pneumatic tyres and a lower steering ratio. The next stage in the development of the Dearborn vehicles was when designs of cars and commercials diverged. This was seen as something of a mixed blessing, due to the fact that spares would no longer be as interchangeable between the two. Chevrolet pulled ahead in terms of sales in 1927, when it produced the best-selling truck in America: this is when the long-standing rivalry between Ford and Chevrolet began. In the same year, Ford discontinued the long production run of the Model T, which had been affectionately known as 'Tin Lizzie', having produced in excess of 15 million.

The Model A Ford

The Model T was replaced by the Model A in 1928, allowing Ford to regain the sales advantage, when the Model A car and Model AA truck began to roll off the production lines. Although Ford had the advantage for the time being, the Wall Street Crash hit America in October 1929 and devastated the economy, leading to the Great Depression, that lasted into the 1930s: it would see an estimated 13 million Americans without jobs by 1932. The Ford Model A car was available in various guises, including a sedan and a convertible. It had a wheelbase of 103in (262cm) and was powered by an in-line four-cylinder 200ci (3277cc) 24-hp engine. This was coupled to a three-speed transmission and the car had four-

wheel brakes. The commercial half-ton AA models were available as both Roadster and Closed Cab pickups and by 1931 there were 31 different colours available.

By 1928, Chevrolet had become a major threat to Ford's domination of both the car and truck markets in the USA. In the last year of the decade, Chevrolet produced its half-millionth truck, and introduced an in-line six-cylinder engine.

Production of GMC trucks had continued throughout the 1920s, with engines supplied by companies including Buick, which also supplied GMC with its six-cylinder engines. Towards the end of the decade, GMC was offering the T-11, a truck based on a Pontiac design that had only been on sale for a single year: even the Pontiac engine was used in this initial model. A new model, the T-19, was introduced in 1928, demonstrating that GMC was also making progress in its truck designs. The T-19 was manufactured in large numbers, and some 20,000 examples were made between 1928 and 1929. Later, GMC would begin to produce Buick engines specifically intended for its trucks, with the bore and stroke altered to make them suitable for use in commercial vehicles. These engines, which were offered in different displacements, were to continue in production for more than 20 years.

Production of Studebaker trucks had not resumed until 1927, when a new model was announced that was subsequently produced until 1931, when the company again abandoned trucks. In 1929, however, IHC sold around 50,000 trucks and the overall market

for pickup trucks appeared to be growing.

The final years of the 1920s saw a new phenomenon developing, that of the suburb. The availability of motor vehicles now meant that people were able to work in the city and live at the periphery, though by now a tax on gasoline had been levied by every state. This would bring about a major shift in lifestyles, even though the Depression was on its way. Early in 1929, the millionth Ford Model A rolled off the assembly line, followed by the two-millionth in July the same year. With mass-production on this scale, there would be a growing source of future raw material for hot rods as the craze got going in earnest over the next decade. Intimations that it had already

begun were evident in California, where auto racing on dry lakebeds was beginning to happen in an ad hoc way. The dry-lakes scene is believed to have started in the middle years of the 1920s, when Frank Lockhart, a Glendale resident, tested his Stutz Blackhawk at Muroc. The Blackhawk was powered by an in-line 95-hp eight-cylinder engine, that could exceed 100mph (160km/h). The homespun view of the hot rod's history is that 'it was created by everyday folks, who took an old Tin Lizzie, stripped off the fenders and hood, and hotted-up the engine, gave it a personalized, unique look, and had a machine that outperformed all the other cars on the street'. One aspect of this is certainly true:

OPPOSITE: This 1926 Model T Ford coupé was one of many body styles offered during the Model T's long production run.

BELOW: The perfect raw material for any hot-rodder: a factory-fresh 1928 Model A Ford two-door sedan.

jalopies, modified, soup-jobs or hot rods (a contraction of 'hotted roadster') – call them what you will, were coming into vogue in California before the advent of the V8 engine. The V8 would literally and metaphorically push things along just that little bit faster.

CHAPTER TWO

THE THIRTIES: THE ARRIVAL OF THE DEUCE

Not many would have been able to afford a new car or pickup in the first years of the 1930s, when the Great Depression was beginning to spread its tentacles far and wide. Following the Wall Street Crash of October 1929, banks began to close their doors right across America, and unemployment was to reach almost five million. In 1930 two million fewer new vehicles were registered than in 1929, and the situation worsened in 1931 as total vehicle production dropped yet again.

In 1932, Al Capone began an 11-year sentence for tax evasion in Atlanta prison, later on Alcatraz, which was all that could be proven against the notorious gangster, while America got its first woman senator, when Hattie Caraway, a democrat, was elected to represent Arkansas. Ford and Chevrolet slugged it out through all of this, even as production totals continued to drop across the industry. In 1932 Chevrolet introduced an in-line six-cylinder engine and Ford responded with a V8, in a year when production would be the lowest in 17 years. As a result of the in-line six, however, Chevrolet sales rose to the extent that it began to outsell Ford, and Henry Ford realized that he had no choice but to go one better and introduce a V8. V8 engines were not new, being already in use in

OPPOSITE: Henry Ford with his flathead V8 engine. Its development was problematical, but Ford's persistence paved the way for the mass-produced V8 engine.

RIGHT: The architecture of early gas stations is now the subject of academic study and some are being preserved. This is an example from the early 1930s.

luxury cars, such as Lincolns, built by Ford since it had bought the company from the Lelands in the 1920s; but they were not available in mass-produced cars and trucks. In view of the economic situation at the time, Ford's V8 was big news indeed.

Also new for 1932 would be the Model B Ford, subsequently nicknamed the 'Deuce', which, despite its launch in a time of austerity, became one of the most famous American cars of the 1930s. One of the main reasons for this is that it came with an L-head V8 engine, though a flathead four was also an option. The V8 gave the Deuce considerable performance that would subsequently endear it to the hot-rod fraternity. It has been said by hot-rodders that the Deuce is one of the few vehicles that looks as good with its curved fenders fitted as it would with them stacked against the garage wall. The Deuce was to become the quintessential hot rod, and a symbol of youthful enthusiasm and American ingenuity. The 1932 Ford's style and performance put it in the forefront of a developing trend towards personalizing vehicles and adding to them aftermarket parts. The V8-powered truck

Fordors were less popular at first, and Cabriolets, convertible sedans and Sport coupés were rarer still. Ford built 12,045 1932 Roadsters and a disproportionate number survive to this day, due to the attentions of the hot-rod fraternity. Production figures were as follows: Standard Phaeton 1,076; Deluxe Phaeton 1,204; Standard Roadster 1,468; Deluxe Roadster 10,612; Standard Coupé 49,246; Sport Coupé 2,721; Deluxe coupé 21,474; Victoria 7,762; Tudor Sedan standard 94,483; Tudor Sedan deluxe 22,913; Fordor Sedan standard 13,426; Fordor Sedan deluxe 21,500; Convertible Sedan 883 and Cabriolet 5,926. Of this total of 253,811 cars, 178,749 were powered by the new V8, while the remainder were powered by the in-line four-cylinder engine.

The 1932 Ford commercial vehicles consisted of a sedan delivery, a Murray and Baker-Raulang-bodied station wagon, and two pickups. The pickups were a Murray-bodied Open Cab and a Closed Cab truck. The Sedan Delivery (with a single side-hung door, rather than a pair as in a panel van), the Station Wagon Woody, and the open-cab pickup were built in small numbers, with production totalling 2,371 for all three, while 14,259 closed-cab pickups rolled off the Detroit line. Most of them were powered by four cylinders, because the V8 was not available for them until late in the model year. The Murray-bodied Open Cab pickup was assembled from parts of other Fords, including Model A leftovers, but the Closed Cab featured a new all-steel body that shared styling and parts with the cars.

Sales of the 1932 models may have been

variant was the Model BB, which also appeared in 1932.

The problem inherent in manufacturing a mass-produced, and therefore cheap, V8 was the difficulty in casting the crankcase block and cylinder banks in a single unit. Up until then, the V8 had been cast in three parts, before being machined and fitted together. Times were hard, and even Ford was obliged to close a number of his autoplants, laying off approximately 75,000 workers as his financial resources became ever more stretched. His patternmakers and foundrymen worked day and night to cast the complex V8 blocks, struggling to control 54 separate sand cores.

At times, the scrap rate was as high as 100 per cent, but eventually the problem was solved, and an affordable V8 became a reality. Of this breakthrough, Henry Ford was able to say, 'The V8 is the coming car for the majority of American drivers. As always, we have done the pioneer work. It will only be a short time until motor manufacturing practice will follow the trail we have blazed.'

The design of the new Ford range progressed under Edsel Ford, Henry's son, and designer Joe Galamb, while the engineer Gene Farkas redesigned the chassis in a way that eliminated the need for splash aprons between the body and running-boards (which

is why the 1932 looks good without fenders). When the 1932 Ford range went on sale, it consisted of ten car variants and four trucks. The car range comprised a Phaeton, a roadster, a standard coupé, a deluxe coupé, a sport coupé, a Victoria, a Tudor Sedan, a Fordor sedan, a convertible sedan and a cabriolet. Phaetons and roadsters were available as standard and deluxe models. Of this range, the Roadster, the Standard Coupé (the five-window) and the Deluxe Coupé (the three-window) were to become rodders' favourites, although the Victoria – known as the Vicky – and the Tudor two-door sedan were also in demand. Phaetons were rare,

OPPOSITE: A 1933 Series 46 half-ton roadster pickup. This is the four-cylinder-engine version, although a V8 option was available.

ABOVE: A 1934 Ford five-window, denoting a standard rather than a deluxe coupé, with aftermarket tyres and wheels.

slow, with Ford making a loss of $75 million, but the new engine was responsible for re-establishing Ford's position as the leading automaker. The depths of the Depression were plumbed in 1933, as thousands of farmers of the Oklahoma dust bowl and surrounding areas, headed west in battered old cars and trucks in search of a better life.

The importance of the car in migrations such as these should not be underestimated. John Steinbeck, writing of the plight of the Joad family, dispossessed tenant farmers fleeing Oklahoma, writes evocatively on the subject in *The Grapes of Wrath* of 1939: 'Limp flags in the afternoon sun. Today's Bargain. '29 Ford pickup, runs good. What

do you want for fifty bucks – a Zephyr?'

Ford's range for the 1933–34 sales season included Sedan Deliveries that followed the lines of the redesigned car range of coupés and roadsters, while the Roadster and Closed Cab pickup models remained nearer in appearance to the 1932 range. Ford managed to stay ahead of Chevrolet in the numbers of trucks sold, although Chevrolet made rapid progress through the 1930s, with hydraulic shock absorbers, vacuum windshield wipers, electric fuel gauges, and external rear-view mirrors becoming standard equipment. Chevrolet had acquired a specialist body-maker for its trucks in 1930, the Martin Parry Corporation, which enabled it to offer a range of half-ton Pickups, Panel Vans and Canopy Express Trucks as factory models. The acquisition of Martin Parry would eventually boost Chevrolet's sales in the light truck market, far beyond the 32.7 per cent it had already achieved by this time.

Throughout the 1930s, Chevrolet offered a range of colours and a synchromesh transmission, pushing its trucks hard by means of fleet sales. All of this contributed to the company's market share, which climbed from that achieved in 1930 to 50 per cent in 1933, the same year that it produced its millionth truck. As the 1930s progressed, Chevrolet trucks became more streamlined, styled in the manner of its passenger cars, and certain models shared the same front-end sheetmetal. The range included trucks of a larger capacity, including three-quarter and one-ton models. Progress continued, and in 1934 Chevrolet trucks came equipped with hydraulic brakes (referred to in the slang of the times as juice-binders), and the cabs were built with one-piece steel roofs. The year also saw an increase over that of 1933 as America began its slow recovery from the Depression.

In 1933 a range of trucks, completely designed by Chrysler, had been introduced. The new range featured an in-line six-cylinder engine, which would endure until the 1960s, and the distinctly car-like styling of the time. During the 1930s International Harvester began to use alphabetical designations for its trucks: the A-series was manufactured between 1930 and 1932, the C- series from 1933 to 1934 and so on. There was no Series B, presumably because Ford was already using a similar designation at that time. Of these trucks the AW-1, for example, was a conventional three-quarter-ton, powered by a four-cylinder engine and available in chassis, panel, pickup, canopy truck, screen-side and sedan delivery configurations. The later Model Cs for 1935 included the C-1, C-10, C-20 and M-3; the C-1 models were the half-ton line in both 113- and 125-in (287- and 317-cm) wheelbases, while the C-10 models were three-quarter-ton trucks on a 133-in (338-cm) wheelbase. The C-20 was a larger truck, based on a 157-in (399-cm) wheelbase with a maximum capacity of around 1.5 tons, while the one-ton M-3 had a 133-in wheelbase.

It was during the 1930s that GMC began mass-production of light trucks in earnest. The early-1930s models had styling comparable with the Fords of the day – cabs had vertical windshields, and hoods were long with louvred sides. The range for 1932 included the T-11 half-ton, T-15 three- quarter-ton, and T-15AA and T-17A one-ton models.

The Ford V8 received praise from unexpected quarters: on 13 April 1934, Henry Ford received a letter from Clyde Champion Barrow of Tulsa, Oklahoma, that read, 'While I still have breath in my lungs I will tell you what a dandy car you make. I have drove Fords exclusively when I could get away with one. For sustained speed and freedom from trouble the Ford has got every other car skinned and even if my business hasn't been strictly legal it don't hurt anything to tell you what a fine car you got in the V8. Yours truly.' Barrow was, of course, half of the infamous criminal duo of Bonnie and Clyde.

Meanwhile, out on California's dry lakes, hot-rodders were racing what were called 'modifieds'. These were the cheapest roadsters to build, and as a result appeared in large numbers, because many of the first hot-rodders were young and poor, though blessed with considerable mechanical ingenuity. The modified usually consisted of the engine, drivetrain and rolling chassis of a car – mostly but not exclusively a Ford – together with the bare minimum of salvage-yard bodywork to cover it and provide a seat for the driver. Many Ford Model T parts were used, because they were easy to find in junkyards in the 1930s. Despite their informal beginnings, the modifieds soon grew into an established racing class at the speed trials held on the dry lakebeds of California's Mojave Desert, at Muroc, Harper, Rusetta and later El Mirage. As the class evolved, some of the modifieds became sophisticated machines, though in the early days, much of the fun to be had was simply escaping to the lakes for a weekend's racing. Many of the racers lived in Los Angeles, approximately 100 miles (160km) south-west of Muroc, the journey taking drivers through the San Gabriel Mountains. At this time, Wally Parks, for example, was racing a fenderless 1927 Chevrolet coupé, powered by a four-cylinder engine that achieved 82.19mph (132.27km/h) in June 1933. In 1937, Wally Parks and Ak Miller, of the Road Runners car club, were among the organizers of dry-lakes meets and were instrumental in bringing all the clubs together.

In 1935 the UAW (United Auto Workers) union was formed and was affiliated to the Congress of Industrial Organizations (CIO). The Chevy truck range for this year included Model EC and EA sedan deliveries, an EB Suburban and various EB pickups, and Chevrolet would add a coupé delivery to the range for 1936, based on the FC-series of passenger cars. A redesigned Ford range appeared in 1935, the year Fords became the best-selling cars and trucks in the USA. The restyle incorporated a new, narrower grille, a longer hood, and more rounded fenders. The design was only slightly revised for 1936, with minor changes to the wheels and radiator grille shell. An unusual Ford truck appeared in 1937 in the form of a standard coupé car with pickup body, introduced to compete with Chevrolet's Coupé Delivery of the previous year. Coupé pickups were poor sellers for both companies, and Ford discontinued them at the end of that same model year, although Chevrolet persevered with its version until the outbreak of the Second World War. Plymouth commercial vehicles were offered between 1935 and 1942 alongside Dodge trucks, as both companies were part of the Chrysler group. Plymouth was the low-cost brand and employed the same strategy to sell its pickups as it did its cars, in which dealers with joint Chrysler-Dodge franchises were offered an opportunity to increase their sales. The first commercials from the company were 'commercial cars' – passenger cars produced with a sedan delivery body. Production was numerically small, but was considered sufficiently worthwhile for the company to increase the range from 1938 onwards.

The year 1937 saw the opening of San Francisco's Golden Gate Bridge to traffic and Studebaker introducing a truck. Studebaker sales were good and the company would remain in the pickup business until the closure of its Indiana plant in 1963. Its 1937 model was the Coupé Express, and borrowed most of its front sheetmetal from the surprisingly named car, the Studebaker 5A Dictator. This truck was based around a 116-in (295-cm) wheelbase, and was powered by an in-line six-cylinder L-head engine of 217.8ci (3569cc). For 1938, the pickup was based on the concurrently-produced car and so featured the same front-end sheetmetal. Once again, for 1939, the pickup was to share its front end with Studebaker's car line, so the truck was restyled again.

133mph in 1938

One of hot-rodding's key dates is 7 February 1938, the day on which the Southern California Timing Association (SCTA) was founded. It unified once and for all the sport of dry-lakes racing, adopting one set of rules that were put into effect on 15 May 1938 at an event at Muroc. The SCTA's rules accommodated two types of race cars: roadsters and modifieds. By the end of 1938, the fastest modified was that belonging to the Spalding brothers. Tom and Bill Spalding achieved 120.5mph (193.9km/h) in a Ford flathead V8-powered car. By 1939 the fastest modified was that belonging to George Harvey, with the Pugh brothers achieving 127mph (204km/h) in 1940. John and Rod Pugh were in different car clubs, the Road Runners and Gear Grinders respectively, and actually competed against one another in the same race. The Pughs' record lasted through the 1941 season, but was broken in what was to become the shortened 1942 season by Karl Orr.

Karl was a mechanic and the owner of a hot Ford Model A Roadster. He met Veda while she was working at the MGM studios, and they were married in 1936. The couple became interested in dry-lakes racing, in which Karl drove the roadster and Veda crewed, and by the time the SCTA had been formed they were heavily involved. Women did not race cars in those days, but one day Veda drove her husband's roadster at a meet, making a secret pass through the clocks. Soon afterwards, Veda turned her attentions to a Deuce roadster, while Karl continued to race his modified. He achieved the modified record in his V8-powered car with a top speed of 133.03mph (214.08km/h). This was a considerable achievement in a single-seat roadster with open wheels and a flathead V8; it was fuelled with pump gas and had been put together with little more than ingenuity. Fittingly, because the SCTA abandoned the modified class in 1947, Orr's record stands to this day. The term hot rod would become

The streamlined and luxurious Lincoln Zephyr Model H V12 sedan was introduced for the 1936 model year. It had a 122-in (310-cm) wheelbase.

popular in the 1940s, but the first examples, called 'gow jobs' or 'soup-ups', were built during the Depression by young enthusiasts, usually with little or no money, who were eager to tinker with what was then still a novel piece of machinery. Many of those early hot-rodders also wanted to show-up their wealthier rivals, to prove that money wasn't

OPPOSITE: The Model 73 Ford half-ton pickup of 1937 was powered by a 60-hp version of the flathead V8. The truck was available as the pickup seen here, and also as a stakebed, platform, chassis and cab, panel-van, and in standard and deluxe trim.

the only way to automotive excellence. Even so, a hot rod has always been a social statement, having more to do with self-reliance, ingenuity, and ultimately, independence, rather than power and performance.

The GMC truck range was redesigned for 1936 and again for 1937, the T-14 of 1937 being a half-ton truck powered by a 230-ci (3769-cc) in-line six-cylinder engine. The front end featured a vertical grille, with bullet-shaped headlights positioned between the fenders and the sides of the hood, while the remainder of the truck was of a basic configuration that would endure for several years. In 1937 almost 35,000 GMC trucks were registered, and the company offered a similar range for 1938, but with the headlights mounted on the sides of the hood. Meanwhile, International Harvester had expanded its truck line in 1936 to include seven basic models within its range – all with styling similar to that of the 1935 models. This included a tall V-shaped grille, long hood with louvred sides, a tall cab and curved fenders that ran back to join the running boards. The smaller-displacement trucks used Waukesha four-cylinder engines, while the larger models used an in-line six.

A redesigned line of IHC trucks – the

D-series – made its debut in the spring of 1937. The appearance of the new models was considerably altered as a result of redesigned grilles and two-piece windshields, and had a fat-fendered appearance. The all-steel cab styling was referred to as 'turret-top' by its maker, and the new range enabled IHC to increase its lead over Dodge and retain third position in sales in the USA, with 30.22 per cent of the total truck market. The figure would drop considerably to only 10.24 per cent for 1938, but would surprisingly still leave IHC in third position. The IHC trucks continued almost unchanged for 1939 and IHC sales improved slightly to give the company 11.38 per cent of the total US market.

There were significant changes at Ford in 1938, when its vehicles came assembled with a chassis that conformed to the specifications of the American Society of Automotive Engineers (ASAE), recommendations which included better brakes and larger-diameter wheels. That year, Ford also offered a range of one-ton trucks to complement its existing half-ton line, and by 1939 Ford trucks were equipped with 'juice-binders'. The range had also been expanded to make it even more comprehensive, with the addition of three-quarter-ton models. These trucks featured a rounded radiator grille shell, even more rounded fenders, and steel wheels instead of the laced wire types used until this time. The Ford Motor Company introduced the first Mercury during 1939, intended as a medium-priced automobile to fill a space in the company's range between

the Ford and Lincoln models. The 1939 Mercury had a 95hp at 3,800rpm version of the 239-ci flathead V8 under its hood and was capable of 90mph (145km/h).

GMC was also aware of the changing trends and its range was redesigned for 1939: windshields now came in two pieces and although the grille remained vertical, it was redesigned to incorporate heavier looking horizontal inserts. The company offered four six-cylinder-powered half-ton models on a 113.5-in (288-cm) wheelbase, and three similarly-engined models with a 123.75-in (314-cm) wheelbase. The half-tonners were designated the Series AC-100 and AC-102 trucks, while the greater payload models were the AC-150, AC-250 and ACL-300. In the various capacities, there were chassis, chassis-cab, pickup and panel-van models, with platform, stakebed and express models in the larger-capacity trucks. For 1939 the Plymouth range included the PT81 pickup, powered by an in-line six-cylinder engine driving through a three-speed transmission. Slightly more than 6,000 of these trucks were produced.

In 1939 Ford of Canada was conscripted into the war effort to build a range of military vehicles. The hot-rodders' favourite engine – the flathead V8 – was used to propel a variety of these machines, including light-tracked Universal Carriers and light armoured cars such as the Ford C29SR Lynx. Even Ford cars, such as the Forty Ford, appeared in olive drab, making them suitable for use as staff cars. A 1941 Ford station wagon was especially built by Ford of Canada for Britain's Field Marshal

Alexander. Known as the C11AD, the roof was chopped off and replaced with a canvas soft top. It was fitted with 13in diameter wheels and sand tyres and was powered by a 95-hp flathead V8.

Hitler's German armies invaded Poland on 1 September 1939 and Canada joined the war in support of Great Britain, which had declared war on Germany a few days later, after the Nazis refused to withdraw their troops from Poland. With an eye to world politics, President Roosevelt declared a 'limited emergency' within a week of the beginning of the War in Europe, and permitted further recruitment into both the US Army and the National Guard. The process had actually started earlier that summer, when the strength of the army had been increased from 175,000 to 210,000 men. General Marshall, recently appointed Chief-of-Staff, established several tactical corps HQs, with enough troops to create a fully functioning field army. He also reorganized the basic infantry into five three-regiment 'triangular' divisions, and aimed to make them more manoeuvrable and flexible. In 1940 the first Corps manoeuvres held since 1918 took place, and these were later followed by Corps versus Corps exercises. While mechanization of the US Army had commenced in 1936, it had been a slow process due to lack of funds. The coming war would soon change that and would also see many hot-rodders wearing olive drab. It would also irrevocably change the entire world in the years that followed, especially in terms of industrial mass-production and automobile design.

CHAPTER THREE

THE FORTIES: WAR & A NEW START

The Ford cars for 1940 were unveiled on 5 October 1939. The story had begun a few months earlier, however, as the new body styling had evolved from the 1938 Deluxe Tudor and Fordor sedans. The lines of the coupé and station wagon were identifiably those of the 1939 models, while the Convertible, Sedan Delivery, Half-Ton pickup and Panel delivery were true 1940 models.

The most obviously new feature of the 1940 Ford was the deluxe grille and hood. It featured a narrow, two-piece die-cast grille centre section, fitted into a louvred sheetmetal frame, designed to fit between the holdover 1939 fenders, while the nose of the Deluxe hood was contoured to match the new grille. The Standard models of the 1940 cars featured a die-cast grille that closely resembled the stamped sheetmetal of the 1939 Deluxe grille. Other styling features included chromed die-cast headlamp frames on the Deluxe, painted on Standard models, and distinctive chevron tail lights. The 1940 models also had windshields set in rubber seals, with a chrome bar dividing the two panes of glass and the dashboards were substantially redesigned. The chassis, with its 221-ci (3621-cc) flathead V8 and leaf springs, was an evolution of earlier Fords. The X-shaped cross member originated from 1933, for example, but aside from

hydraulic brakes – juice-binders – it was the column gearshift that was the innovatory feature of the 1940s models. As Ford said, it was 'finger tip gearshift in all models at no extra cost'. What made this car important is that within a few years it was another Ford car that would be highly sought by hot-rodders. In fact, as early as July 1941, a picture of a Standard Coupé, taking part in a speed competition, could be seen on the cover of *Throttle*, one of the early hot-rod magazines.

It is generally acknowledged that the Ford range for 1940 comprised some of Ford's most distinctive cars and trucks. The trucks featured styling similar to that of the cars, that year, with a graceful hood that came forward to finish almost in a point. The rear sheetmetal varied, depending on the type of vehicle in a range, and included panel van, pickup and

LEFT: This nostalgic Ford T has a Southern California Timing Association decal in the lower corner of the windshield.

OPPOSITE LEFT: Three carbs set up on top of a V8 engine was a popular tuning trick of hot-rodders.

OPPOSITE RIGHT: The dash instruments are aftermarket parts, as is the steering wheel.

stakebed trucks. There were half-, three-quarter- and one-ton variants, with wheelbases of 112, 122 and 122in (284, 310 and 310cm) respectively. The coupé pickup reappeared for 1941 and the radiator grille and hood designs varied in the trucks according to their payloads. Marmon-Herrington offered a 4x4 conversion in the three-quarter-ton Model 11D Pickup, while Willys Overland was producing similarly-styled cars and trucks with hoods that finished in a point at the front. The vehicles had progressed from flat grilles with the introduction of the Model 77 in 1937, that became the Model 38 in 1939 and the Model 441 in 1940; in the latter year, the company produced a total of 32,930 cars and trucks. By

1940 Plymouth was offering the PT105 pickup truck, which closely resembled the Dodge trucks of the time. It was powered by an in-line six-cylinder engine of 201.3ci (3299cc) displacement, that produced 79hp at 3000rpm. The truck was based on a 116-in (295-cm) wheelbase chassis. The slightly upgraded models for 1941 became the PT125-series; these pre-war models were to be the last trucks from Plymouth for 33 years.

Ford became unionized on 21 June1940, but the development in industrial relations was generally overshadowed by world events. While war raged in Europe, America was initially an uneasy bystander. In 1940, however, the US Army was able to procure

much-needed motor transport. The reason for this was in part the reorganization of the army, in which it was intended that non-divisional cavalry, in the form of cavalry recce squadrons, should ride 'point' ahead of the new divisions. A squadron would consist of three recce troops and nine recce platoons, that would be transported in a defined number of White Scout cars, Dodge Command Cars and motorcycles.

Meanwhile, Bob Rufi was the first to exceed 140mph at the lakes. He drove an aluminium-skinned streamliner at 143.54mph (230.99) at Harper's Dry Lake on 10 May 1940, making it one of the greatest pre-war achievements in the realms of speed.

Pearl Harbor, December 1941
Japanese air strikes on Pearl Harbor, Hawaii, and on Guam and the Philippines on 7 December 1941, propelled America into the Second World War, following an Act of Congress passed on the day immediately following the airstrike. Within days, the US Marine Corps was fighting a desperate action in defence of Wake Island, a tiny Pacific atoll that, until that point, had been used by Pan American Airways to refuel the huge flying boats it used on its around-the-globe services. The lead story in numerous editions of US newspapers told how for 16 days the Marines had made a determined stand against overwhelming odds. It was also the first

intimation, so soon after the disaster of Pearl Harbor, that although the road to victory would be long and massively costly, America, the most powerful industrial nation on earth, would ultimately win. When America eventually joined the war, its massive industrial capacity firmly supported the war effort, and companies previously known for making civilian cars, such as Willys and Ford, were soon making Jeeps. Truck-makers turned over their production lines to military trucks, while other companies began to make tanks.

For owners of private cars, however, driving was becoming progressively more difficult during 1942. Production of civilian passenger cars came to an end on 9 February, with that of civilian pickups ceasing on 3 March, while a national speed limit of 40mph (64km/h) was imposed to conserve gasoline. This was later lowered to 35mph, and gasoline rationing was finally introduced at the beginning of December. In early 1943 the Office of Price Administration banned all non-essential driving in 17 eastern states, and by 1944 fuel had been rationed to two gallons per car per week. By the end of 1944, the Americans had produced 88,410 tanks, which was a triumph in terms of mass-production techniques.

On 4 March 1942 the War Production

Board issued a stop order on Willys-Overland's automobile production, and Willys turned its full attention to the quarter-ton 4x4 Jeep MB. Ford's civilian trucks were redesigned for 1942, before the company began to concentrate its efforts on winning the Second World War. Another of Ford's contributions to the Allied cause was to turn some of its production capability over to building Willys MB Jeeps; this is because Willys did not have the vast production capacity required for the task. The Ford-assembled Jeeps were designated Ford GPW and the company also produced an amphibious variant, which was designated GPA. By the time war ended, Willys had built 358,489 MB Jeeps and Ford 277,896 GPWs.

All Chevrolet plants participated in the war effort, with the exception of Saginaw, that continued to make spares exclusively for the civilian Chevrolets already on the road, while towards the end of the war, Studebaker was permitted to produce some pickups for essential civilian use. Meanwhile, Chrysler made Sherman tanks and Pontiac produced anti-aircraft guns. In 1945, following the

OPPOSITE: The body is channelled – lowered over frame rails.

ABOVE: A current fashion is for basic rat rods, such as this bare-bones Model A.

RIGHT: The Chevrolet V8 has long been a popular engine for hot rods.

OPPOSITE: This early-style hot rod, based on a Ford Model T, is simple yet stylish.

LEFT: This triple-carbed Chevrolet V8 offers performance and nostalgia.

abandon its Lend-Lease Studebaker trucks, when all that was wrong were fouled spark plugs. Studebaker assembled almost 200,000 US6 two-and-a-half-ton 6x4 and 6x6 trucks, with half of these going to the USSR as Lend-Lease equipment: Russia itself produced a close copy of this truck in the post-war years at the GAZ plant in Gorky. The US Army maintenance units sandblasted plugs night and day to keep vehicles running, and when they ran out of sand, men were sent to the landing beaches for more, even . though it had to be dried and sifted before it could be used.

Ambrose also quotes Captain Belton Cooper's recollection of the war: 'I began to realize something about the American Army I had never thought possible before. Although it is highly regimented and bureaucratic under garrison conditions, when the Army gets in the field, it relaxes and the individual initiative comes forward and does what has to be done.' This initiative was demonstrated nowhere more clearly than in the Normandy countryside during the summer of 1944. It transpired that a weakness of the mass-produced Sherman tank, used for fighting in between the hedgerows, was its underside, which was not as heavily armoured as the rest – a weakness that was exposed in the course of events. Hedgerows were obstacles

Victory in Europe, the US automakers were allowed to resume civilian production that recommenced in July.

By now, many GIs were more familiar with automobiles than the soldiers of other combatant nations, and while by no means all were hot-rodders themselves, they were certainly able to bring something of the hot-rodders' ingenuity to the task of war. As Stephen E Ambrose puts it in *Citizen Soldiers* (Simon and Schuster 1997), 'Kids who had been working at gas stations and body shops two years earlier had brought their mechanical skills to Normandy, where they replaced damaged tank tracks, welded patches on the armor, and repaired engines. Even the tanks beyond repair were dragged back to the maintenance depot by the Americans and stripped for parts.' Ambrose went on to compare the approach of the Russian Army, that as often as not would

that could be easily defended, but were difficult for infantry to cross, and the Americans needed to breach them to let tanks and infantry through. Mechanical ingenuity discovered a solution: Lt Charles Green, a tanker in the 29th Division, devised a fender

from the salvaged railway track the Germans had used as obstacles on beaches, while Sgt Curtis Cullen of the 2nd Armored Division, a mechanic from New Jersey, designed and supervised the construction of a similar device made from scrap metal taken from a German

roadblock. These allowed the Shermans to bulldoze their way through the hedgerows and make holes for the infantry to pass through, without exposing their undersides. Cullen's device became known as a Rhino and the Shermans that were so-equipped were known

OPPOSITE: Early modified lakes influences are evident here in this minimal racer.

ABOVE: This period-perfect nostalgic rod uses a 1927 Ford T body, Ford wire wheels and Ford flathead V8 engine.

as Rhino tanks. It was such an obviously good idea that to this day, many tanks are equipped with a bulldozer blade.

Wally Parks and Eldon Snapp were also US servicemen, and were the brains behind the SCTA. Parks was a test driver of tanks for General Motors, where he drove M5A1 light tanks powered by twin Cadillac V8s, driving through a Hydramatic transmission. He was drafted in 1943 and Veda Orr took over

responsibility for the SCTA publication, working with a mimeograph machine in the corner of Karl's speed shop. As the war progressed, Veda Orr assumed the task of sending the magazine to 750 GIs around the world. Each month, the SCTA news carried information about their readers who were now in uniform, and kept morale high and dreams of racing on the lakes alive. It is difficult to imagine just how much the arrival of the

magazine meant to someone in a foxhole in Italy or isolated on a Pacific island.

Racing on the dry lakes resumed after the war, and many racers now had more than a few dollars in their pockets, which meant that as well as the wartime improvements made in technology, hot rods inevitably got hotter.

In 1948, Veda Orr took her flathead-powered roadster to seventh place in the hotly-contested C/Roadster class, which

ABOVE: A matt black Ford roadster with a flathead engine, no hood, and Firestone whitewalls is about as nostalgic as it gets.

OPPOSITE: A gathering of old-time hot rods at Hemsby, gives a glimpse of what it was like in California in the 1940s.

required consistent speeds in excess of 120mph (193km/h). She went on to self-publish the first hot-rod book, *Veda Orr's Lakes Pictorial*, which contained a history of the early days of dry-lakes racing and portrayed the California hot-rod scene from an insider's point of view. Possibly as a result of the increasing availability of V8 roadsters, entries diminished in the modified class, and during the 1946 season there were between ten and 15 entries per meet; consequently, the

SCTA abandoned the class, preferring to concentrate on the streamliner class that became the lakester class in 1949. A technological development that benefited the lake racers was the use of streamlined war-surplus aircraft 'belly' tanks as car bodies, another being the development of custom wheels; the Halibrand Company – the first to make such wheels – was formed in 1947.

Wally Parks was instrumental in reactivating the SCTA, and served as its

general manager between 1947 and 1949. He was very nearly the first to achieve 150mph (241km/h) in 1948, when he ran at over 148mph; at the same meet, however, Howard Wilson, driving Stuart Hillborn's streamliner, beat him to the magic number. Parks went on to become the first editor of Bob Petersen's *Hot Rod* magazine and with Petersen and Lee Ryan met representatives of the State of Utah, with a view to opening the Bonneville Salt Flats for an annual speed week. A one-time

permit was issued to the SCTA for 1948 and the official Bonneville Speed Week began.

Hot Rod magazine was a landmark development in the evolution of hot rods and street rods. Although the sport was by now two decades old in California, it wasn't widely known outside the state, though this was quick to change following not only the return of GIs from war, but also the fact that *Hot Rod* was now available nationwide. The magazine fast gained credibility because it was staffed by writers and photographers, who themselves were involved in rodding: in other words, it practised what it preached. From January 1948, *Hot Rod*'s editorial philosophy was based on showing its readers, in an entertaining manner, how to build and where to drive hot rods. The magazine hired editors who were involved in the hot-rod scene and who could articulate, within its pages, the various processes needed to start and complete a car. At first, the magazine focused on the dry lakes, land-speed attempts and track roadsters, but soon took in the street action too, until it eventually covered almost all forms of modified vehicles. *Hot Rod*'s first issue featured Eddie Hulse on its cover. Hulse had recently set a new SCTA class record at the El Mirage dry lake, with an average speed of 136.05mph (218.94km/h) in a Class C roadster. This first issue also included advertisements for Navarro Racing Equipment, for heads and manifolds from Glendale, California, and for Riley Racing Carburetors from Los Angeles, California.

Alex Xydias was born in 1922 in Los Angeles, California, and his first car was a 1929 Model A Roadster with a tuned engine.

LEFT: A nostalgic modified roadster.

BELOW: This basic Model A roadster is an evocation of an earlier age.

OPPOSITE LEFT: This nostalgic Model T rod is cleverly detailed.

OPPOSITE RIGHT: Six gauges fill the dash panel of this roadster.

earned a place in history with the So-Cal streamliner. This was an aluminium-bodied machine, a joint effort between Batchelor and Alex Xydias, that was the fastest car in the US, having blown through the lights at 193 and 210mph (311 and 338km/h) in 1949 and 1950 respectively. Xydias and Batchelor's streamliner featured on the cover of issue 22

After he graduated from Fairfax High School, he took a job pumping gas in a local gas station, allowing him to fund his second car, a 1934 three-window coupé, which was followed by a 1934 convertible. After the war began, he worked in a factory making recoil mechanisms for cannons, but in September 1942 he enlisted in the US Army Air Corps, where he was an aircraft maintenance man at Luke Field in Phoenix, Arizona. He returned home after the war and opened the So-Cal Speed Shop which, by his own admission, was difficult at first, but perseverance eventually paid off. In 1948 the shop's V8 lakester clocked 136mph (219km/h) and the company's flamboyant streamliner, powered by an Edelbrock-equipped Mercury V8, achieved 210mph (338km/h) in 1950.

Dean Batchelor was another Californian hot-rodder who returned from war with a thirst for speed; he had been a crew member of a B-17 bomber, known as 'Flak Happy'. This was shot down over Munich, Germany, and the crew was sent to a German POW camp. As the Russians advanced, Batchelor, together with thousands of other POWs, was forced by the Germans to march west for 80 days, covering 500 miles (805km) to the American lines, where the column's guards surrendered to the US Army. Back in California in 1945, Batchelor bought a 1932 Ford roadster and built a hot engine for it, with a Mercury block, an Edelbrock intake manifold, a Clay Smith camshaft and Navarro heads. This roadster became a racer as well as a vehicle that was used everyday, but he

illustrates the close links between street rods, dry-lakes racing and drag-racing, it also shows the beginnings of their divergence. One had to be a club member to run at the lakes and although the Vultures were charter members of the Russetta Timing Association (RTA), its membership was dwindling fast, so George joined the Rod Riders from San Pedro. He built another roadster, but by this time a competitive lakes car was no longer street-legal, and racers such as Bentley gravitated away from street rods to concentrate on lakes racing. One of his major tasks was to drive Evans' purple-and-white flathead-powered belly-tank at the lakes, Bonneville and Daytona.

At a Second World War airbase-turned-airport in Goleta, north of Santa Barbara, a group of Santa Barbara and Ventura rodders began to use a network of abandoned roads on the north side of the base, to tune up their cars on Sunday afternoons during 1948. Some of these, including the Motor Monarchs club from Ventura, approached the airport manager to see if they could run legal drag races on the property. Agreement was forthcoming on the condition that the events were insured. The group named itself the Santa Barbara Acceleration Association (SBAA) and began to hold organized events every other Sunday in 1948 and 1949. Stopwatches were used to time the quarter-mile, and there were three classes: roadsters, fenderless coupés and coupés with fenders.

of *Hot Rod* magazine in November 1950.

Street racing also boomed in the Los Angeles region in the immediate post-war years, when it seemed as though every neighbourhood had a drive-in with a street-racing venue nearby. In Long Beach, it was one of the highways that radiated from the Los Alamitos traffic circle, while in El Monte it was Fifth Street and Turkey Valley: on the westside, it was Culver Boulevard and in east Los Angeles it was Ferguson Drive. East Los Angeles was home to the Vultures car club, and one of its members was George Bentley. In 1946 he equipped a 1932 Ford with a hot flathead V8 for street-racing, and he and a friend took it out to Scribner's drive-in in Culver City one Thursday night, which was

when street-racing took place. Bentley's buddy ended up driving the 1932 in an impromptu race on Culver Boulevard but lost control, ending up upside-down, escaping uninjured, but spending eight weeks in jail. All that was salvageable from the wreck was the engine and driveline that Bentley fitted to his next car, a chopped 1931 coupé on Deuce rails. Towards the end of the decade, Bentley found himself driving one of Earl 'Pappy' Evans' cars: Evans was the proprietor of Evans' Speed Equipment in Whittier, California, and for the next ten years Bentley drove for Evans at the lakes, Santa Ana Drags, Bonneville and even at Daytona. The fact that a street-racer could race on the lakes as well as in the fledgling drag races not only

Money for trophies was raised by passing a hat around and adding in a percentage of the takings from the burger van. It is reported that 50 cars would run each weekend and a similar number of spectators showed up to watch. The Goleta events petered out in 1951, due to the fact that there were other strips in existence, the Korean War had started, and the SBAA had itself grown tired of running the events.

In 1947 the San Diego Prowlers Hot Rod car club was formed, when a bunch of rodders got together and drove their cars up to the lakes, making local hot-rod history by running in the time trials for many years. Over time, the Prowlers began to hold car shows, a tradition that continues to this day. The tradition of the San Diego Prowlers holds that its cars must be pre-1948 Ford cars or trucks.

George Barris was born in Chicago in the 1920s. In 1928, he and his older brother, Sam, moved to Roseville, California, to live with relatives after their parents died. The brothers were diligent students and George pursued his passion for building model aircraft and cars. The parents had given the boys a 1925 Buick in need of repair, in exchange for work done in the family restaurant, and the Buick became the Barris brothers' first custom car. The Buick needed considerable attention and the duo made it look quite different. They straightened the body and added accessories, and George hand-painted the car orange with

Two different styles of Ford rod: the Hiboy roadster (opposite) and a chopped and channelled coupé (left).

blue stripes. It was eventually sold to enable them to buy a 1929 Model A. Their interest in cars increased during their teenage years, as they began to hang out at local bodyshops after school, and George had created his first full custom from a used 1936 Ford convertible by the time he graduated from high school. Shortly afterwards, George formed the Kustoms Car Club, the first time this spelling was used. After Sam enlisted for the duration of the Second World War, George moved to

Los Angeles, where he opened his first shop in the Los Angeles suburb of Bell in late 1944, with Sam joining him after his discharge from the military in 1945. They then opened a new shop on Compton Avenue in Los Angeles, which was known as the Barris Brothers' Custom Shop. Here, Sam's prowess at metal working complemented George's desire to design and paint. George began to race at Saugus Speedway in around 1947; this was short lived, however, as the brothers'

business expanded and took up all their time.

The first Hot Rod Show, promoted by Robert 'Pete' Petersen, founder of *Hot Rod* magazine, was announced around that time, and the Barris brothers were asked to exhibit the only custom car in the show. New automotive magazines, including *Hot Rod*, were now being published giving full coverage to the business of custom cars. George Barris began to photograph and write for the magazines, and was simultaneously

OPPOSITE: The Russetta Timing Association was one of the organizers of dry-lakes racing in the 1940s.

ABOVE: The sleek lines of this 1934 three-window are enhanced by hot-rod modifications, such as a roof chop and the removal and modification of the fenders.

able to promote his business by describing custom techniques in a step-by-step form.

The Auto Industry Gears Up

The war had seriously interrupted the work of the auto manufacturers, as it had in every other walk of life. Most of the major manufacturers' 1946, '47 and '48 model-year trucks were essentially nothing more than slightly improved pre-war machines. For its immediate post-war trucks, Ford kept the design features of the last pre-war models, including the so-called 'waterfall' grille, described thus because of its row of vertical bars. In 1946 GMC resumed civilian production with light trucks that were almost

ABOVE: A hopped-up four banger, in Model A five-window form, at the drags.

RIGHT: The nostalgic rodding scene thrives today.

OPPOSITE: A cool-looking 1927 T-based hot rod with Deuce grille shell.

identical to the pre-war models: this was designed to allow its staff more time to design a new series of light trucks. International Harvester's civilian production also fully resumed in 1946, with the reintroduction of the K-series. These trucks were redesignated the KB-series, when they were redesigned for 1947. Little had changed

from the pre-war models and little would change until 1950. After the war, Studebaker reintroduced its pre-war M-series trucks as 1946 and subsequently 1947 and 1948 models. As a result of experience gained in wartime mass-production in 1947, the company produced more than 67,000 trucks, a figure that exceeded the total number of trucks that had been produced pre-war.

The new post-war GMC models were to be the FC-series, and featured GMC's all-new 'Advance-Design' styling, which was smooth and rounded overall, while the grille comprised a series of horizontal bars, and a GMC logo was affixed to the hood above the grille. The headlights were mounted in the fenders, which complemented the streamlined appearance. Because the new design of truck had been introduced part-way through 1947, it continued to be marketed through 1948, and with only minor improvements to the design, continued into 1949.

Chevrolet trucks were similarly comprehensively redesigned for 1947 – described by Chevrolet as Advance-Design – and now incorporated rear-hinged hoods in a redesigned cab with such innovations as a column shift. Sales generally boomed in the post-war years, and 260,000 Chevrolet trucks were sold in 1947. The new 1947 design was sequentially upgraded, with vented windows, new door latches, a redesigned grille, and a

OPPOSITE: Scallops, as painted on this Model T, are one of the earliest custom paint styles.

ABOVE: An authentic-looking 1940-style rod, based on a 1927 Model T.

new autobox: the first two were introduced in 1951 and 1952 respectively, and the last two in 1954. During this period, Chevrolet offered half-, three-quarter and one-ton pickups on 116-, 125.25- and 137-in (295-, 318- and 348-cm) wheelbases respectively. Pickups were offered in the following configurations in each capacity class: Chassis, Chassis/cab, pickup, platform and stake. In addition, there were half- and one-ton Panel vans and Canopy wagons. The three series were designated 3100, 3600 and 3800, the numbers increasing according to payload and wheelbase. The numerical designations continued for 1948,1949 and into the 1950s. While the overall appearance of the various models remained the same, there were minor upgrades from one model year to the next.

Ford's first post-war range of trucks made the news in 1948. These were the famous F-series trucks – the so-called 'Effies', that ranged from the half-ton F-1 to the three-ton F-8, and endured for more than 50 years. For 1948, however, the styling had been radically altered from what had gone before: now the headlights were set into the recessed horizontally-barred grille, and the fenders were more squared-off and joined across the top of the radiator grille below the hood. The cab was larger in all three dimensions than before and was rubber-mounted to the chassis. The new half-ton truck was known as the F-1 and was available as the F-2 and F-3 as a three-quarter-tonner.

The all-new post-war Dodges also appeared in 1948 in the form of the Series B models. The B-1-B was a half-ton, the B-1-C a three-quarter-ton and the B-1-D was a one-ton. The company made a number of upgrades and options available throughout the 1950s, including automatic transmissions, column-shifters, grilles, and instrument panels. It also upgraded the styling of the cab and a variation on the cargo box was also offered.

CHAPTER FOUR

THE FIFTIES: HOT-RODDING'S CLASSIC ERA

In California, in the 1950s, it was de rigueur that a hot rod be an early Ford, and to be especially cool, a 1932 Ford or Deuce, which should have the spare tyre, the fenders and the stock tail lights removed, and the grille cleaned up. Big and small whitewall tyres were mounted on red-painted steel rims of a corresponding size, and headlights of a smaller diameter than stock-sized were fitted, the fashion dictating that Deuces be lean, mean and clean. For some reason, 1933 Fords weren't that popular, but as for the 1932s, it was a similar story as far as the 1934 Fords were concerned, and no extra garbage was allowed. The 1936 Ford was the only hot rod allowed to keep its spare wheel, but it had to be lowered and flattened against the trunk. The 1936 Ford also benefited from De Soto fenders and a roof chop, which made it a big bucks car in the 1950s, when $150 for a roof chop was big money. The 1935 Fords were not popular and rodders stuck with 1933 and '35 cars usually swapped the front sheetmetal for those of

RIGHT: The 1932 Deluxe three-window coupé had rear-hinged 'suicide' doors.

OPPOSITE: A lowered stance and whitewall tyres give this roadster a 1950s look.

OPPOSITE: The Mercury lead-sled craze started in the 1950s, encouraged by people like George Barris.

ABOVE: Fitting 1939 Ford tail lights to an earlier Ford roadster was a popular 1950s styling trick.

1934 and '36 models respectively. Running boards were also removed and wheels were changed. The wire-spoked Ford wheels had gone out of fashion by the beginning of the 1950s: now, the one-piece steel wheels, introduced in 1940, had become the most popular extra for a state-of-the art hot rod. The tail lights were usually replaced by flush-fitting units, two popular types being the 1950 Pontiac and 1939 Ford teardrop units. The intention of hot-rod builders was to use the best equipment, not always from the same brands, to build an open-wheeled, wind-in-the-hair, powerful car. They were intended to be fun and exciting and a source of pride to a car-obsessed teenager.

In April 1950, a wildly chopped 1934 Ford Coupé appeared on the cover of

Hot Rod magazine. It had run at 142mph (228km/h) at El Mirage, at an event sanctioned by the Russetta Timing Association. By then, most were referring to 'hotted roadsters' as 'hot rods', which sounded cooler and altogether racier. Lakes cars could be roadsters, modifieds, lakesters and streamliners, though the SCTA would not allow coupés, because it was believed that, being heavier, they could not be made to go as fast as the lighter roadsters. However, Dick and Bob Pierson, and their friend and engine-builder Bobby Meeks, from the Coupé Club of Inglewood, would change all that. They decided to build a radically chopped 1934 Ford coupé, powered by a 267-ci (4375-cc) Mercury flathead V8 engine, bored and stroked to produce this displacement. Driven by Bob Pierson, it

became the fastest closed car in America; in 1949 it ran 142.98mph (230.09km/h) and soon afterwards turned 153.06mph (246.32km/h) at Bonneville and also put Vic Edelbrock's performance parts on the map. This was at a time when hot rods were rarely

LEFT: The Pierson Brothers' coupé was one of America's most influential hot rods. It set records, looked great, and proved coupés could be faster than roadsters.

ABOVE: The coupé is now owned by Bruce Meyer and is displayed at the Petersen Automotive Museum in Los Angeles.

OPPOSITE: It's a million miles or more from this radically low, rat-rod pickup.

painted, but the trio turned the coupé out to a particularly high standard, 'because sport car guys sneered at hot rods'. Consequently, it was finished like the Midget cars and Indy racers. The car was still being raced in 1991, when Bruce Meyer bought it and had Pete Chapouris restore it to 1950 specifications: it is currently exhibited at the Petersen Automotive Museum in Los Angeles.

The 1950s in America was a troubled decade: the Korean War began in June 1950, when North Korea invaded South Korea across the 38th parallel, the line by which Korea had been arbitrarily partitioned in 1945. In response to the outbreak of war, the US Department of Defense reactivated the Ordnance Tank Automotive Center in Detroit, Michigan, with a view to mobilizing the automotive industry to war production. On 15 January 1951, Dodge began to build trucks for a military contract, and other automakers also received similar contracts of one sort or another. All-in-all, more than eight million cars, trucks and buses were produced in the USA in 1950, estimated to be more than 75 per cent of all the vehicles made in the world that year. The Korean War continued into 1951, as the People's Republic of China sent troops and assistance to Communist North Korea. In order not to

OPPOSITE: This radically chopped and channelled pickup has a nostalgic appearance.

LEFT: This Chevrolet V8 is neatly detailed: note the modified pistons used as air intakes on the triple-carb set-up.

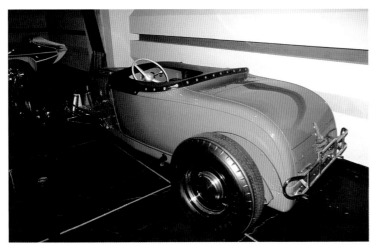

raise the stakes too high, President Truman sacked General MacArthur, the UN Commander-in-Chief, when he talked of invading China. The escalation led to restrictions on the amounts of certain metals, including zinc, chromium, tin and nickel, that could be used in the American auto industry, except when related to defence: Chrysler and Cadillac were now making tanks, and GMC truck plants were assembling the M-135 6x6 truck for the US Army. Numerous other restrictions came into force as a result of the conflict, the National Production Agency (NPA) limiting both car and truck production in order to ensure a continuous flow of equipment for the war effort. The NPA assigned a quota of vehicles to each manufacturer, based on their percentage

LEFT & BELOW LEFT: One of the many famous roadsters in the Petersen Museum. The car is exceptionally detailed.

BELOW: Midget racers influenced hot-rodders.

OPPOSITE: One of the many variations on the Mercury lowrider theme.

PAGES 72 & 73: Flames, whitewalls, hubcaps and furry dice say 1950s, though big and little tyres suggest the three-window is a later interpretation of that theme.

market share, Dodge's NPA quota, for example, being 13 per cent of the industry total. The Korean War dragged on through 1952, the year that the Republican Dwight D.

Eisenhower was elected president, and ended only after the agreement at Panmunjon in July 1953. The cost of the war had been great, with 51,000 Americans dead and the face of world politics changed. The Korean War had been the first confrontation between the big powers in the nuclear age, and was a model of brinkmanship for the numerous Cold War conflicts to come.

The F-series trucks had carried Ford into the 1950s on a very firm footing, and Ford was now the nation's number two automaker, partially as a result of a serious labour dispute at Chrysler, that had affected production. The F-series underwent a redesign in 1951, when a new grille was fitted. In 1952 Ford made two new overhead-valve engines available, an in-line six, and a

ABOVE: Lakes racers painted sponsors' names on their hoods, which helped promote the companies' reputations.

ABOVE RIGHT: The So-Cal Speedshop 1932 roadster in the workshop.

RIGHT: So-Cal Speedshop's streamliner and roadster, shown side by side.

OPPOSITE: An old-time five-window coupé rod with unchopped roof.

V8. The major facelift, however, was saved for 1953 and Ford's Golden Anniversary, being its most radical redesign in two decades. Most significant from the truck-buyer's point of view, was the fact that the F-

series was given the three-digit designations that have been used ever since. The F-1 became the F-100, the F-2 and F-3 became the F-250, while the F-4, slightly downgraded, became the F-350. This seems straightforward enough, but there was a total of 194 models, with numerous options, in the Ford truck range. As the new model, the F-100, or 'Effie', as it was increasingly known, was introduced on 13 March 1953 with a sleeker, more modern appearance than before. It was available in many variants, the F-100 being the one-ton model, available as platform, stake truck and stepside, as the F10D3 straight-six-powered unit, or the F10R3, which was the V8-powered version. Larger-capacity versions were the three-quarter-ton F-250 and F-350.

Ford was making innovations in an area of vehicle design that was still relatively new, that of safety, with tubeless tyres, safety

ABOVE: A bare-bones Model A pickup with flathead V8 power.

OPPOSITE: Painted steel wheels with trim rings and hubcaps, chopped windshield frame, and custom louvred hood give this roadster a 1950s flavour.

OPPOSITE: A modern interpretation of 1950s styling, but with a modern twist, makes this three-window a great rod.

LEFT: Scallops, hubcaps and angled windshields are 1950s features, while big and little tyres and show-standard paint are more recent innovations.

steering wheels, better door locks and a shatterproof rear-view mirror. These inexpensive upgrades, however, failed to be a sales incentive, but only ten years later, government regulations were to force such measures on the US automotive industry. It was intended that the all-new GMC and Chevrolet ranges of 1955 model trucks

should go on sale alongside the redesigned car line in the fall of 1954, but the scale of Chevrolet's model-line revisions, sales pressures from Ford, and contracts arising from the Korean War, forced the company to delay the introduction of the new line until April 1955: the first series of 1955 trucks were slightly upgraded 1954 models, that

were on sale from August 1954 until March 1955. In 1954 America tested the first aerial H-bomb on Bikini Atoll and something else occurred that would have a bearing on America's future. This was the agreement that partitioned Vietnam into North and South, and recognized both Cambodia and Laos as independent nations, following the

end of French rule in what was formerly French Indo-China. The mid-1950s Federal programme of interstate and freeway building within the US also caused a shift in automobile buying patterns: demand increased for higher-performance cars, which meant that the large-displacement in-line six and V8-powered models were becoming ever more popular.

In the 1950s, Lions was a famous dragstrip in Southern California, known as LADS, Long Beach or simply 'the beach'. It was situated off Freeway 405, and operated from 1955 to 1972. There were others, such as Colton, that operated from the middle of the decade until the mid-1960s, and Santa Ana, reputedly the first commercial dragstrip. It used a spare runway at Santa Ana airfield in return for ten per cent of the profits from every event. At first, entry was 50c, but later it increased to 90c plus 10c tax. There were up to 200 cars running each weekend and the events drew many spectators. These drag races were organized by C J 'Pappy' Hart, who was probably responsible for standardizing the races over the quarter-mile; he got the idea of this from sprint events in which Quarter horses took part, and quarter-mile drags soon became universal. Expansion eventually precluded drag racing on the

LEFT: Two contrasting examples of 1950s-style 1932 Ford roadsters.

BELOW: Rodders wearing 1950s-style clothes are often seen at nostalgic events.

OPPOSITE: With roof chop, scallops and whitewalls, its hard to believe it's not a 1955!

District Court decreed that nine black students be allowed to enrol in the previously segregated Central High School. Orville Faubus, the segregationist Governor of Arkansas, went as far as mobilizing the National Guard to block the school to the black students. There were racist mob riots and after a degree of vacillation, Eisenhower send in US paratroopers to restore order. That same year, the first of the sputniks, the world's first artificial satellites, went into

airstrip, and Hart went on to run races at Taft near Bakersfield and later at the Riverside and Lions strips, before going to work for the NHRA. The famous Pomona dragstrip also has its origins in the 1950s: in 1951 the Choppers car club and a Pomona motorcycle cop, Bud Koons, staged weekly drags at Fontana airport, and later in the year moved to a freshly-paved strip at the edge of the LA County Fairgrounds. By 1953 they had acquired a small timing stand, speakers, and hay-bale 'guard rails'. In the San Diego area in the same year, a group of around 20 hot-rod clubs banded together to form the San Diego Timing Association, staging drags on a former US Navy landing strip near National City, known as Paradise Mesa.

The idea of hot rods and drag racing

spread quickly: as early as 1951, Smartt Field, an abandoned Second World War airfield in St Charles County, Missouri, attracted hot-rodders from the St Louis area, who raced on Sundays. Strips eventually emerged all over the Midwest, in locations such as Alton, Illinois; Great Bend, Kansas, and Milan, Michigan. Others included the Mid-America Raceway near St Louis, the Great Lakes Raceway in Union Grove, Wisconsin, and Quad City Dragway in Cordova, Illinois.

The latter part of the 1950s were banner years for auto manufacturers, but seriously troubled ones in other respects. In 1957, events in Little Rock, Arkansas, brought international attention to the civil rights cause. The crisis erupted when a Federal

OPPOSITE: A neat pickup brings a novel approach to its use of flames and chequered firewall.

LEFT: Boat-inspired Duvall windshields were a custom touch used in hot-rod roadsters in the 1950s.

these imports firmly embued with street and strip performance styling and a degree of beach and surfer-inspired style to create a scene that thrives to this day.

Cats Who Build 'em
In 1952, Alex Xydias fitted one of his So-Cal V8 engines to a belly-tank racer, with a chassis built by Dave Langton, the result being a car that realized more than 140mph (225km/h) at Bonneville. Xydias also contributed to a chopped coupé, running a blown 258-ci (4228-cc) Ardun-Mercury, campaigned by himself, Buddy Fox and Tom Cobb, at dry-lakes and drag strips. Using ten per cent nitro, it ran 132mph (212km/h) at the drags.

There had always been a degree of acrimony between hot-rodders and aficionados of sports cars, especially in racing circles. In 1953 Ak Miller built a hot rod especially for La Carrera Panamerica, a frenetic 2,000-mile (3200-km) race across Mexico. This was first run in 1950 and by 1952 was dominated by European sports cars. Miller had raced an Oldsmobile in the race in 1952, and was able to use his race experience and mechanical ingenuity for 1953. His car consisted of a 1927 Model T roadster body on a narrowed and shortened 1950 Ford chassis, powered by a 324-ci (5309-cc) Oldsmobile

orbit, heralding the beginning of the space age. In recognition of the fact that such new technology would certainly have its spin-offs in the automobile industry, various manufacturers produced futuristic concept vehicles: GMC's truck and coach division rolled out the Turbo-Titan, an experimental truck designed and built to use a gas turbine engine for power, while Ford produced the similarly experimental Glidaire, that travelled on a cushion of air rather than wheels. Ford took the idea a step further, and followed the Glidaire with the Levacar that, like the Curtiss-Wright Aircar, was also an air-cushioned vehicle. By 1959 Chevrolet, as part of GMC, produced the Turbo Titan II, a second gas turbine-powered truck, while Chrysler experimented with an electro-chemical source of power, and Cadillac experimented with radar for cars. A clue to future developments also came in 1957, when the first imported Volkswagen trucks and vans took to America's highways. The VW would spawn its own sub-culture, which would see

V8. In the wake of the race, *Motor Trend* magazine's Don Pope wrote: 'Ak Miller grinned whenever you saw him, like a guy who didn't know he was carrying on his shoulders the hopes and fears of thousands of cats who build 'em instead of buy 'em. Ak didn't outrun any Lancias or Ferraris, but he outlasted plenty of the $20,000 jobs. It really was a sight to see Ak bowling along with the

biggest and best in the business. Came in eighth, he did.' Miller returned in 1954, and after 1,908 miles (3070km), finished seventh overall and fifth in class. This was achieved in a car estimated to have cost $1,500 and a lot of sweat.

During the second half of the 1950s, another hot-rodder, Frank 'Duffy' Livingstone, a Second World War combat flight engineer,

raced a 1920s Ford chassis with a 1924 Model T body in sports car events. The hot rod was originally powered by the almost ubiquitous Ford flathead V8, but it was later replaced with a Chevrolet small-block engine. The dated-looking hot rod, driven by Livingstone, was capable of beating Porsches and Maseratis, but only provoked scorn from sports car owners. In 1959, at a USAC event

OPPOSITE: Driving a nostalgic roadster pickup in the sunshine – it doesn't get much better than this!

ABOVE: A 1927 Model T, with late-model tail lights, pinstripes, chopped windshield and whitewalls on steel rims, makes this example 1950s-perfect.

at Pomona fairgrounds, he qualified 19th in a 57-car grid. During the race, he was able to climb as high as eighth before finishing in 11th place. The car survived, and is now owned by Brock Yates; it was restored by Pete Chapouris for an appearance at the Amelia Island Concours d'Élegance of 1991. Later, it made its first race appearance in years at the 1997 Monterey Historic Automobile Races, driven by Bert Skidmore. The car followed its previous form and tore through the field of exotic sports cars to an eighth-place finish. This was followed by an appearance at Pebble Beach concours.

In 1955 George Bentley drove the NieKamp-Peterson D Modified Roadster to become a member of the 200-mph club at the lakes, with a two-way average of 203.338mph (327.232km/h). In October 1957 *Hot Rod* magazine, now billed as 'Everybody's Automotive Magazine', cost 35 cents per issue, and featured on its cover a 1932 three-window, with two swimsuit-clad girls proclaiming the hot rod to be 'America's true sport car'. In March 1958, the cover featured a 1927 T hot rod, that shared space with a group-testing of new Dodge, Chevy and Ford pick-ups. From 1956 until 1964, Californian 'Flathead' Jack Schafer raced some of the fastest flathead V8-powered dragsters of all time, including a 296-ci (4850-cc) rail and a 1941 G/Gas 322-ci (5277-cc) Willys coupé. He is now the proprietor of Flathead Jack's – a supplier of Ford V8 flathead engine parts.

There is a period-perfect 1950s-style 1932 roadster in the Henry Ford Museum in Dearborn, Michigan. It was largely built and owned by Dick Smith from Arizona, and from 1955 to '61 was his only means of transport. The museum wanted to buy the car to star it in an exhibition showing the influence of the car on American culture and history. For the 1950s part of the exhibition (the era of drive-ins, 45rpm records, Dwight D Eisenhower and James Dean), the curators deemed an authentic 1950s hot rod to be essential, and after looking long and hard chose Smith's roadster. Smith had bought the metallic-blue car, already a rod, from another Phoenix rodder, Bob Cline, who had removed the fenders and fitted the flathead Mercury V8 in the late 1940s. Smith repainted the car gloss black in 1954, after his discharge from the US Army, and rebuilt the car while he was at Arizona State University. He combined the 1932's frame rails with a 1942 X-member, fitting a Bell front axle and a 1940 Ford rear, with 3.54 gears in the differential and a Chrysler 331-ci (5424-cc) Hemi mated to a Packard transmission. This set-up also incorporated a Winfield cam, Challenger intake manifold, home-made headers, and the clutch and flywheel from a 1950 Dodge pickup. Because the car was built in the 1950s, long before the advent of aftermarket parts, suitable parts had to be found; Smith used some war surplus aircraft parts in his rod, which included the pedals, switches and rear-view mirror, while the windshield was shortened to enhance the low, sporty look. Later, new radius rods were fabricated for the front axle and new side-panels for the hood. It is a classy embodiment of the 1950s, when cool hot rods were the result of their owners' ingenuity and ability, rather than the size of their wallets.

This museum hot rod is typical of many that cruised cities and towns throughout America during the decade. It is typical of the iconic style that many teenagers and young men were looking for, when they built and modified their own vehicles, with components taken from other cars. The accent was on high-performance engines and on bodies that had been made lighter to improve acceleration; they were given modified suspension to improve handling, which entailed skilled workmanship in modifying and machining parts and mating them together in an unorthodox but creative manner. By such means, a car became uniquely identified with its creator. Part of the point of the exercise was to display one's own craftsmanship, while 'cruising' showed the car off, and impromptu and highly illegal races on public roads, or races at legal drag strips, demonstrated the car's ability.

Around this time, the Barris brothers outgrew their shop on Compton and moved to a larger one in Lynwood, where the famous Hirohata Mercury was built. Sam Barris had bought the two-door Mercury new, well aware that it would make a great custom. Bob Hirohata admired its style and donated his 1951 Mercury for the custom treatment. Barris finished the car in order to show it at the 1952 Motorama, where it turned out to be the star of the show. George Barris established the Kustoms of Los Angeles club, that was initially restricted to Barris customers: it grew out of the weekend custom runs that George helped promote, but later became Kustoms of America. Kustoms of America is still a thriving club that now organizes a major

OPPOSITE: This flathead V8-powered roadster, with its matt paint, artwork and steel wheels, is inspired by hot-rodding's dry lakes-racing era.

annual cruise in Paso Robles, California.

Various movie studios had taken note of Barris Kustoms and approached George Barris for subjects for their films. One of the first movies for which Barris built cars was *High School Confidential*, the success of this venture into the world of movies encouraging Barris to seek his fortune in Hollywood. Shirley-Ann Nahas, George's future wife, is now an integral part of the success, since Sam Barris left the business, and George has been concentrating on promotion as well as customizing. He has travelled all over the country in his cars, attending car and custom shows and appearing on talk shows on TV.

In the late 1950s, Revell began making model kits of his cars. AMT saw were the trend was going and offered a plastic model of the Ala Kart show car, plastic model kits being huge-selling toys at the time. Meanwhile, original customs and hot rods continued to roll off Barris's drawing board. They were built and decorated by the best fabricators and craftsmen in the business, including Bill Hines, Lloyd Bakan, Dick Dean, Dean Jeffries, Von Dutch and Tom McMullen. As the 1960s dawned, Barris moved to a new shop in North Hollywood, where he continued to design and build award-winning and spectacular cars. examples that became famous in TV shows were the Munster Coach, the Batmobile and the Monkeemobile.

CHAPTER FIVE

THE SIXTIES: GASSERS & MUSCLE CARS

Dan Dare spaceship-style fins were still in evidence on American sedans as the 1960s began, and hints of similar styling could be seen on trucks. By now, the USA produced almost 48 per cent of all automobiles worldwide. In 1960 US automakers produced 7,869,271 vehicles of which 6,674,796 were passenger cars. It also imported 468,312 cars and exported 322,561. In that year it was estimated that 90 per cent of US intercity travel was made by automobile.

The early years of the 1960s were troubled ones for the American nation. There was the fiasco of the Bay of Pigs, in April 1961, when an attempt was made to oust Fidel Castro, and the following December, James Davis was the first American serviceman to be killed in Vietnam. Less than a month later, on 12 January 1962, parts of Vietnam were defoliated by the US in Operation Ranch Hand, using the chemical Agent Orange to accomplish the task, while heightened Cold War tensions precipitated the Cuban Missile Crisis in October 1962.

Hot-rodding was still very much intertwined with drag racing, and the 1960s are remembered for the dragstrip 'gasser wars'. One of the most famous gassers of the era was the 1941 Willys of Stone, Woods and

Cook, which broke the national B/Gas record on its first outing at California's Lions dragstrip in early 1961. Despite the sport's continuing popularity, in 1961 Alex Xydias closed the doors of the So-Cal Speed Shop, when bigger mail-order companies began to take the lion's share of the business. In any case, Xydias' other business enterprise, that of making motorsport documentary films, was thriving and taking up most of his time.

The decade had got off to a good start for Chevrolet, when it became America's number one truck-maker in 1961, albeit by the narrow margin of only 3,670 trucks over those of Ford, Chevrolet's production

representing 30.39 per cent of the market share. The C-10 was one of a series of 185 trucks made by the company in 1960. Such a massive range was achieved by having many different wheelbases, as well as a variety of optional engines and transmissions, the K-prefix models being 4x4 variants of the C-series. The trucks had been redesigned to include a new grille with repositioned headlamps. The fenders, body sides and hood were redesigned and a sculpted line was added to either side of the body. The range included the half-ton Series 1000, the three-quarter-ton commercial, the Dubl-Duti Series 2000 models, and the one-ton Series 3000.

Minor styling changes brought the line into 1961 and a restyled hood took it forward into 1962. Changes to the styling were kept to a minimum for 1963, but a coil-sprung front-suspension arrangement was introduced at the same time on the 4x2 C-series trucks. The eight-millionth Chevrolet truck was produced in 1962 and the El Camino appeared as a mid-sized pickup, similar in configuration to the Chevelle automobile. By now, production at Chevrolet's plants was in full swing and a further million trucks had been produced by 1964.

In 1960, factory production lines were churning out large automobiles, such as the

Chrysler Valiant, Chevrolet Impala, Dodge Dart, Ford Galaxie, Ford Thunderbird, Oldsmobile 88 and Plymouth Fury. In 1961, US automobile sales were slightly down, with 6,542,000 sales; Chrysler abandoned the

OPPOSITE: This chopped five-window example looks like a tough customer, with its slotted alloy wheels and Chevrolet V8 engine.

ABOVE, LEFT & RIGHT: George Barris built the Ala Kart from a 1929 Model A pickup in the early 1960s; it won the America's Most Beautiful Roadster trophy at the Oakland Roadster Show.

OPPOSITE: The 1960s was the era when a good deal of hot-rodding took place at the drag strip. It was also the era of high-riding gassers.

RIGHT: Hot-rod styles of the 1960s evolved from those of the 1950s, but with new influences.

De Soto name and the sleek, experimental Plymouth XNR roadster was exhibited in the same year. In 1962, the year Ford introduced the Fairlane, sales fell again to 6,250,000, but increased to 7,644,403 in 1963, when Chevrolet contracted the Italian stylists Nuccio Bertone and Pinin Farina to restyle the Corvair into the Testudo and Monza respectively.

In America's Deep South, racial tensions came to a head in 1963, when a number of black civil rights workers were murdered in Alabama and Mississippi. In almost a repeat of the Little Rock incident of 1957, George Wallace, the segregationist Governor of Alabama, mobilized the National Guard to prevent two black students from taking their places at the University of Alabama in Tuscaloosa, with the result that the National Guard was removed from the control of the state. In August 1963, Martin Luther King made his historic speech at the Lincoln Memorial in Washington, DC, while in November, John F Kennedy, President of the USA since 1960, was assassinated in Dallas, Texas, causing shock waves across the globe. Vice-President Lyndon Baines Johnson, who had accompanied Kennedy on the trip to Texas, was subsequently sworn in in Dallas as the 35th President of the USA.

There was a famous dragstrip in

Southern California in the 1960s, the Fontana, which closed in 1972, while another was at Ramona, approximately 30 miles (48km) north of San Diego, its official name being the San Diego Raceway, though it was generally referred to as Ramona. Drag racing was big news in the 1960s; bands sang songs about drag racing and street rods, and drag-race cars were looking less and less like street cars. By now, Detroit's automobile factories had become involved in racing, and as the sport became more and more legitimate, more classes were established; by the middle of the decade, even the Funny cars could be seen on the strips. Out on the streets, styles were an extension of those of the 1950s, though George Barris and Ed Roth were branching into wild show cars, while Pontiac heralded the beginning of the muscle-car era by fitting a Tri-Power 389 engine and a GTO badge to the Tempest saloon. *Hot Rod* magazine of April 1965 was practically a *Who's Who* of aftermarket performance parts, with advertisements for

the Moon Equipment Company, E T Mags, Mickey Thompson Equipment, Sun Electric Corporation, B&M Automotive, Edelbrock Equipment Company, Engle Racing Cams, Halibrand Wheels, Joe Hunt Magnetos, and Crower Cams. Now, editorial features kept readers up to date with news of the 1965 NHRA Winternationals drag meet at Pomona, and the AHRA Winternationals at Scottsdale, Arizona. Meanwhile, at the Pomona meet, the Stone, Woods and Cook 1941 Willys gasser lost to K S Pittman's 1933 Willys Gasser, and Pittman's Willys coupé also won the Little Eliminator class in Arizona with a 10.10- second 141.06-mph (227-km/h) pass. Hot rods that made the magazine included a twin-Chevy V8-powered 1923 T, a 1928 Ford Roadster pickup, and a five-window Model A coupé.

The decade of the 1960s was a time of transition for street-rodding, due to the arrival of 'factory hot rods' in the form of the GTO, 409, 4-4-2, Stingray and XKE, while family cars now came with racing stripes and horsepower ratings featured prominently in advertisements. This era of muscle car versus street rod was touched upon in the film, *American Graffiti*, where the hero in the chopped 1932 five-window ends up racing a tough 1955 Chevy. Drag boats, dune buggies and go-karts were also becoming popular, while fashions in street-rodding were beginning to change; for a

OPPOSITE: This street-driven 1932 roadster shows dragstrip influences, especially big and little tyres on American Racing Equipment wheels.

ABOVE: This high-riding 1932 roadster dragster has the look of 1960s' cars.

LEFT: Willys coupés and pickups from 1941 (one of the latter is shown here) have long been popular as bases for dragstrip gassers.

OPPOSITE: This chopped 1932 five-window example has classic 1960s street-rod style, enhanced by its tyre and wheel combination.

while, narrow-band whitewall tyres on steel rims, with hubcaps and 'beauty-ring' trims, were popular. With hindsight, the transition from 1950s hot rod to 1970s resto rod was already becoming evident.

Ford set the Mustang loose on the world in 1964, while Chevrolet launched the Chevelle in 1964 and in 1965, looking towards the future, built another futuristic concept truck, the Turbo Titan III, with a gas turbine engine for power. It was displayed at auto shows, and two years later Dodge unveiled its concept truck, the Deora. The Dodge Deora was fitted with an internal combustion engine but offered car-like comfort in a pickup. In many ways, these vehicles were anticipating sport-utilities by at least 15 years. Despite Chevrolet's use of a gas turbine engine in its concept machine, its internal combustion engines had plenty of miles left in them, and in 1965 truck registrations exceeded the 500,000 level. It was a boom time for America's number one truck-maker, and a year later its ten-millionth pickup was sold.

The market for the recreational pickup user grew rapidly during the mid-1960s, bringing with it changes to the ranges offered by manufacturers such as Chevrolet who, in 1965, introduced a 325-ci (5326-cc) V8-

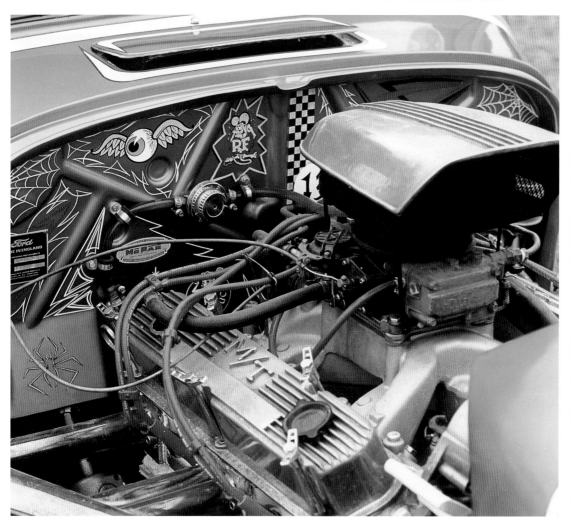

OPPOSITE and LEFT: The firewall artwork with 'flying eyeball', and the spider's-web grille, is reminiscent of the 1960s styling of Von Dutch and Ed Roth.

powered long-box model, suitable for a demountable camper fitment. They also introduced a camper special, which had a beefed-up power train and chassis components. International Harvester was also aware of the growing recreational market for utility vehicles: a 1965 survey of buyers of IHC Scouts showed that around 75 per cent had been purchased for non-business use and 82 per cent of them were in 4x4 form. The US commitment to South Vietnam was also expanding during the mid 1960s. In March 1965, two Battalion Landing Teams of the US Marine Corps were the first ground combat troops to be committed to Vietnam: by 1966, the Vietnam War had cost America $5.8 billion.

The Early Times Club was formed in California in the mid 1960s to preserve street-driven rods. The club hosted its first annual picnic in 1965, since when it has become a street-rod institution that endures to this day. Another institution of a similar age is the annual LA Roadsters Father's Day Show, held at Pomona, California, while Darryl Starbird's show, held at the fairgrounds in Tulsa, Oklahoma, has been an annual affair since 1964.

Chevrolet's trucks were redesigned for

1967, and optional interior packages, including the CS and CST were also offered. Chevrolet regarded this redesign as 'the most significant cab and sheetmetal styling change' in its history, and certainly the trucks acquired a much more 'modern' appearance, seeming longer and lower and much closer to the styling of cars of the time. This was the result of the trend towards pickups for personal transportation and leisure vehicles, as well as for working vehicles. The trucks were redesigned to slant inwards above the waistline and to incorporate a swage line that defined the wheel-wells and body-sides. The area of glass in the windshield and side windows was increased and the elongated appearance was reflected in the grille, that featured two long, narrow rectangular panels. The new C-10 was offered on two wheelbases in both Fleetside and Stepside forms and as either a 4x2 truck or a 4x4. The only noticeable change for 1968 was the addition of more badges and chrome trim to the trucks. Hot on the heels of this redesign in 1969 came the Blazer, Chevrolet's first full-sized 4x4. The suspension arrangement on the Blazer was to use tapered single-leaf springs at the front and multi-leaf springs at the rear. The 4x4 Blazer base model was powered by an in-line six-cylinder engine, although V8s were optional. There was a choice of manual or automatic transmissions, and power steering, power brakes and a removable fibreglass hardtop were optional extras. Colours, exterior trim, interior trim and general equipment were not dissimilar to those of the K-10 4x4 pickup models.

This was what the mainstream automakers were up to, but of more interest to rodders was the fact that Andy Brizio, trading from a shop in San Francisco, was now building cars. The Instant T, that did much to popularize the Fad T – a street-rod version of a 1923 Model T, was so extreme that it seemed like a caricature of the Model T. In general, the Ts had buggy spring front suspension, coil-sprung rear suspension and a rectangular-section tube chassis, topped off with a fibreglass body from a Model T. Brizio built cars for the 1968, '69 and '70 Oakland Roadster Shows and won the coveted America's Most Beautiful Roadster trophy in 1970. He followed the Model T buckets with a Model T C-Cab van (so-called because of the profile of the rod's door apertures).

Meanwhile, war was still raging in Vietnam and the US Army was consuming 850,000 tons of supplies and 80 million gallons of gasoline monthly by 1967. At the end of January 1968, the Viet Cong launched the Tet Offensive against Saigon, Hué and other South Vietnamese cities, and places such as Khe Sanh and Da Nang were being committed to the pages of the history books. By 1969 the USA had spent $28.8 billion fighting the Vietnam War.

Even *Hot Rod* magazine was touched by the war; on page 47 of the November 1968 issue was an advertisement for the army that read, 'Vietnam. Hot. Wet. Muddy. Perilous. To prove yourself here is to prove yourself to the world. No test is harder. No trial more demanding. But when a man serves here, he proves himself a man. To his country. To

himself. Your future, your decision… choose Army.' The magazine's more normal fare included advertisements for Autolite batteries, Wynn's, Ford, Edelbrock, Valvoline, Sunoco, Remington shavers, Gunk, Plymouth cars, STP, General Motors, Pennzoil, the 1969 Oldsmobile 4-4-2, Crower Cams, Hurst, Lincoln-Mercury, Harley-Davidson, Union 76 oil, American Motors, 1969 Buicks, Goodyear, Pontiac, Shelby Accessories, BSA motorcycles, Coca Cola, the Z28 Camaro, Uniroyal, Crane Cams, B&M, Hedman Hedders, Holley, Offenhauser, Jardine Headers, Moon, Keystone, Engle Racing Cams, Cal Custom, Hooker Headers, AC and Gulf – a veritable A to Z of American and imported automobilia. Editorially, the magazine was its usual mix of performance how-tos, feature cars and event reports. Noteworthy among pre-1948 cars were a Model T pickup and an Austin Bantam AA/Fuel Altered dragster, while mention was made of the NHRA Nationals' drag meet of 1968 and of a 1932 three-window street rod. The fact that the cover story had been devoted to the forthcoming Baja 1000 illustrates the growing popularity of off-road and desert racing.

It was a similar story in early 1969, the year that saw Neil Armstrong and Buzz Aldrin land on the moon – a major achievement in the space race for the USA. This began in 1961, when the Russian cosmonaut Yuri Gagarin was the first man to conquer space. Overshadowing this, however, was something else in which the US had become embroiled, and seemingly

could not win: the Vietnam War. In May 1969 units of the US Army and South Vietnamese forces attempted to take Hill 937 – Hamburger Hill – in the A Shua Valley, east of the Laotian border. This turned into one of the bloodiest battles of the Vietnam War and provoked heavy criticism, the hill being of little strategic value.

Earlier on, the January 1969 issue of *Hot Rod* magazine featured a smattering of street rods, including two Model A roadster pickups. There were also plenty of images of early iron running at Bonneville, interspersed by advertisements for both the US Army and Ed 'Big Daddy' Roth's 1969 't-shirt catalogue for 75c'. To these were added test reports of stock factory muscle cars and drag-race results. Bikes had won the second annual Mexico Baja 1000 race, while the duo of Larry Minor and Jack Bayer in a Bill Stroppe-prepared Ford Bronco made it the first four-wheeled machine to finish the race.

OPPOSITE: A 1960s-style Ford Model A sedan – note the hubcaps and whitewall tyres.

CHAPTER SIX

THE SEVENTIES: RESTO RODS & TWO-TONE PAINT

In Vietnam, on 5 September 1970, Operation Jefferson Glenn began. It was fought in Thua Thien Province by troops of the 101st Airborne Division (Airmobile) and units of the South Vietnamese 1st Infantry Division, and was to be the last major military operation in Vietnam, in which US ground forces took part; it would not end until October 1971.

It has frequently been suggested that the design of American automobiles reflects the mood of the country at a particular time, and

LEFT & BELOW: The resto rod came into vogue in the 1970s, the intention being to create a standard appearance with stock lights and spare wheel, but with a modern V8 engine under the vintage tin.

OPPOSITE: The alloy wheels in this 1970s-style coupé are a clue to its hot-rod underpinnings.

the idea does appear to have some credibility. Truck and car styling had been flamboyant in the euphoric post-war years, but looked

decidedly lacklustre in the uncertain years of the mid 1970s. The decade would also see President Richard M Nixon scaling down and subsequently ending US involvement in the Vietnam War, having been faced with ever-increasing opposition to the war at home and abroad.

Meanwhile, US automakers were now operating numerous assembly plants around the world, with 50 in South America, 60 in Europe, 17 in Africa, 40 in Asia and 27 in Oceania. Although these figures would have shifted significantly by 1973, there was concern about the volume of US domestic auto production, when compared with the number of imported vehicles. In 1970 imported vehicles numbered more than 2,000,000, while domestic factories produced in the region of 8,200,000. This latter figure represented 15.9 per cent of America's steel, 41.2 per cent of its iron and 8.2 per cent of its aluminium production.

In 1971, Apollo 15 put a wheeled vehicle on the moon, when astronauts James Irwin and David Scott drove the Boeing-constructed roadster, the Lunar Roving Vehicle (LRV) several miles over the moon's surface, while closer to home, the trend towards trucks for recreation was growing ever stronger. In 1972 the popularity of

LEFT: Panel vans, such as this, made particularly popular rods during the 1970s.

OPPOSITE: Carol Smith's 1930 Ford has wide wire wheels, a popular street-rod component in the 1970s.

OPPOSITE: This 1934 Ford Woody may appear almost stock, but it is a street rod through and through.

RIGHT: This gasser, owned and raced by Al O'Connor, is a long-standing dragster that has been raced in the US and Europe.

mobile homes, camper trailers, truck campers, travel trailers and truck covers was such that a rise in pickup sales was recorded as part of the surge in recreational vehicle (RV) sales. Pickups were used to haul trailers and carry camper bodies, and it was noticed that the average RV family, which consisted of four members headed by a white collar worker, spent 10 per cent of its time using the vehicle. This was quite different from the pickup, whose driver would most often be a blue collar worker, using the vehicle for industrial or agricultural purposes.

The gas crisis of 1973 brought the muscle-car era to an abrupt halt, and many enthusiasts found other vehicles to modify, including vans and Volkswagens, since when the Volkswagen scene has matured and endures to this day, while the van scene fitted neatly alongside the growing popularity of RVs. In what was possibly a reaction to the run-of-the-mill cars coming out of the factories at the time, massive flared fenders and multicoloured metalflake paint jobs were suddenly de rigueur. In 1971, as rods again began to appear out of the woodwork, the Nor-Cal Early Iron Car Club was founded, street-rodding began to re-emerge, and it seemed as though the scene had suddenly got its second wind.

The Fastest Car in the Valley
The National Street Rod Association (NSRA) Nationals began with the first event in 1970 in Peoria, Illinois, and were held annually in Memphis, Tennessee in 1971; Detroit, Michigan in 1972; Tulsa, Oklahoma in 1973; St Paul, Minnesota in 1974; Memphis, Tennessee in 1975; Tulsa, Oklahoma in 1976, America's bicentennial year; St Paul, Minnesota in 1977; Columbus, Ohio in 1978; and St Paul, Minnesota in 1979.

Street Rodder magazine was launched in 1972, and in 1973 rodding received an unexpected boost from Hollywood, when George Lucas' *American Graffiti* hit the silver screen – a nostalgic look at the California hot-rod scene. *American Graffiti* is an affectionate coming-of-age tale, the action taking place during a summer night in 1962. It follows four high-school friends, poised on the threshhold of adulthood. The young cast included Richard Dreyfuss as Curt Henderson, Ron Howard as Steve Bolander, Charles Martin-Smith as Terry the Toad, while John Milner was played by Paul Le Mat and Harrison Ford was Bob Falfa, the out-of-towner in the street-racing 1955 Chevy.

Besides the Chevy, other cars included a 1951 Mercury, a 1958 Impala and John

LEFT: The Fad T was a product of the 1970s, given a boost by the likes of Andy Brizio of Andy's Instant T, San Francisco.

OPPOSITE ABOVE: Popular in the UK, the Ford Anglia was the basis of many 1970s street rods and dragsters.

OPPOSITE BELOW: This Fad T uses a 1923 Model T 'bucket' body and shortened pickup bed.

Milner's 'piss yella' 1932 Deuce coupé street rod – 'the fastest car in the valley', and were stars in their own right. All were period-perfect, especially the five-window 1932. The movie's producer, Gary Kurts, paid $1,300 for the coupé, having chosen it because its top had already been chopped. It was fully-fendered, had a Chevy V8, and black tuck-and-roll upholstery, and was taken to Johnny Franklin's shop in Santa Rosa to complete its transformation. The front end was rebuilt and chrome-plated, new headers were made up, a Man-A-Fre intake was fitted, with four Rochester two-barrel carbs, while a T10 four-speed transmission was installed to drive the Chevrolet's back axle. The rear fenders were bobbed, the front fenders were replaced by cycle guards, the grille was sectioned, and the entire car resprayed canary yellow. In this guise, it was one of the most famous cars of the 1970s. Universal Studios eventually sold the coupé, and it is now owned by Rick Figari, who had longed to own it ever since he saw it in the movie when he was eight years old.

On 27 January 1973, the signing of the Peace Accords in Paris, France, brought the Vietnam War to an end. It had been the longest war in American history and the nation had lost in excess of 58,000 men, killed or missing in action. The war had not only significant socio-economic effects on the nation, it also precipitated the resignation of a president and the political turmoil that followed.

Sales of light trucks began to taper off during 1973, due to the 'gas crisis' caused by the Arab oil embargo. Although this would hasten the trend towards smaller, more economical vehicles, during this period, Chevrolet produced a truck powered by a 454-ci (7440-cc) V8, and managed to sell its 15-millionth truck: nevertheless, Ford was still able to regain the lead in sales from Chevrolet. Now, the biggest threat to the Ford Motor Company was no longer Chevrolet, but the compact trucks being imported from abroad.

That year, the Japanese companies, Datsun (later Nissan) and Toyota, were selling their Li'l Hustler and Hilux trucks. The latter was based around a 101.6-in (258-cm) wheelbase and weighed 2,480lb (1125kg). Toyota's Hilux was powered by a water-cooled in-line four-cylinder overhead-camshaft engine, that displaced 120ci

(1966cc) and produced 97bhp at 5,500rpm. These compacts sold well because of their low price, and both Ford and Chevrolet recognized the need to match them. Ford sourced a Mazda truck from Toyo Kogyo of Japan, described it as the Courier, and badged it as a Ford. The Courier was built to Ford specifications and had rubber mounts between the cab and chassis frame. It was powered by an in-line, four-cylinder, water-cooled 74-hp engine, connected to a four-speed stick-shift transmission. The Courier had a payload of 1,400lb (635kg) and a load bed larger than those of its competitors of the time. In 1972 Isuzu of Japan supplied its mini-pickups to Chevrolet, badged as Chevy

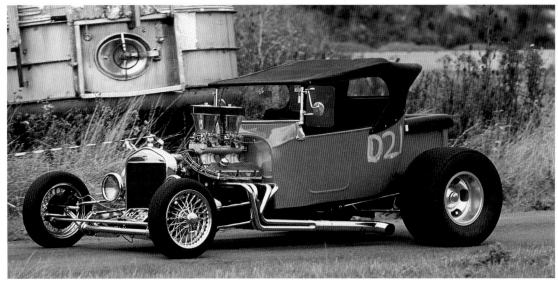

LUVs. The LUV designation was an acronym for Light Utility Vehicle, but at the same time had the ring of 1970s slang. More than 21,000 LUVs were sold in the period between March and December 1972.

Chevrolet offered its half- and three-quarter-ton trucks with a 4x4 option from 1973, the year of its 15-millionth truck. Interior trim was now offered in the Custom, Custom Deluxe, Cheyenne and Cheyenne Super range. Sales topped the 920,000 mark, and despite the gas crisis, the 454-ci engine was enthusiastically received. The following year, the interior packages were renamed Silverado and Scottsdale, which enabled Chevrolet to dominate the 4x4 light-truck market. Chevrolet's full-sized pickups were completely redesigned that year, the new design featuring squared-off wheel-arches, sculpted body-sides, a roomier cab with a greater area of glass, and an egg-crate-style

radiator grille. Trim levels included Custom, Custom Deluxe, Cheyenne and Cheyenne Super. For 1974, a full-time 4x4 was available in the four-wheel-drive models through use of the NP203 transfer case in V8 models: The in-line six-cylinder engine was unavailable in California, due to its emissions regulations. The 400-ci (6555-cc) small block V8 was added to the list of optional engines for 1975 and the NP203 transfer case became standard on all V8 automatic transmission models, while the manual models retained the conventional part-time system with locking hubs. In the interior, the Custom trim level was discontinued, leaving the Custom Deluxe as the base trim.

The year 1974 saw the first NSRA Nationals East held in Timonium, Maryland. It was also the year of the Watergate scandal and President Nixon's resignation, as the US Congress sought his impeachment, and Gerald R Ford became the 38th President of

OPPOSITE: The 'classic' Fad T uses a combination of vintage parts and the necessary modern ones, such as a modern V8 engine and huge rear tyres.

ABOVE: Fad Ts vary, but usually have certain key components in common, including a Model T roadster body, skinny front wheels and wide rear ones.

ABOVE LEFT: A simple but eye-catching Model T street rod, with earlier influences.

LEFT: A Fad T based around a 1927 Model T body with rear turtledeck.

OPPOSITE & LEFT: This Fad T is based on a 1923 T body and shortened pickup bed, powered by a beautifully presented blown V8 engine.

PAGE 112: Another example of a standard show Fad T, built with similar components.

PAGE 113: Imported cars, such as Fiat Topolinos and US-made Austin Bantams, were often used as dragster bases.

the USA. The year was a more auspicious one as far as the nation's truck-makers were concerned. Dodge had redesigned its trucks at the beginning of the 1970s to incorporate independent front suspension, lower and wider cabs, and a new interior. The list of available options was increased, an industry-first being the 'club-cab', an extended-cab model. The grille was redesigned for 1974 and the Ramcharger, a 4x4 Sport Utility, was launched. Innovation continued through the 1970s, with full-time 4x4 systems, a 4x2 Ramcharger and a dual rear-wheel arrangement option for one-ton pickups of 1975 and 1976.

At Ford, production of both the Bronco and Ranchero continued with only minor changes to their design. The styling of the F-100, F-250 and F-350 remained unchanged, but a model with an extended cab was made available, known as the SuperCab. This was available in all three payloads and almost 30,000 were produced in the first year. Ford production of the 1974 range, which had been introduced on 1 September 1973, exceeded the one-million mark for the calendar year, and surpassed that of

Chevrolet, allowing Ford to retain its position as number one. Ford offered 4x4 variants of both the F-100 and F-250 in the same year, following on with the F-150, a half-ton truck, which became available in 1975, while a 4x4 variant of the F-150 followed in 1976.

International Harvester's Scout went forward into 1974 unchanged, while the pickups were given new designations, the half- and three-quarter-ton becoming 100 and 200 models respectively. IHC's pickups remained in production until 1975, when the line was discontinued, as was the Travelall model. Production of light trucks by Plymouth had been halted on the outbreak of the Second

World War and was not resumed until 1974, when the company released the Trail Duster. This was a slab-sided vehicle, typical of trucks of the time, and available as an open machine with a choice of either a soft top or a fibreglass roof. The 1974 model was available with a 106-in (269-cm) wheelbase and was a 4x4, powered by a V8 with an automatic transmission; this had a number of shift positions for off-road use. A 4x2 variant of the Trail Duster was introduced in 1975, featuring independent front suspension in place of the driven live axle. The 4x4 model continued as before, though minor trim and colour changes were made and a 'sport package' was offered as an option at extra cost.

Street is Neat
While the automakers were looking to the future during the 1970s, the popular 'resto rod' style was coming to the fore: it involved giving a rodded car a vintage look, so that wide, wire-spoked wheels, pinstripes, mirrors, spare wheels, luggage racks, fenders and other stock-type components now adorned the steel bodies of earlier cars. While many were able to capture the look, others featured loud paint schemes that in hindsight were possibly too garish. There were important developments in other areas, and new-style rod runs began to appear alongside NSRA Nationals. One of these was held in the small and remote town of West Yellowstone, to prove that the cars,

now increasingly being described as street rods, were capable of being driven long distances. Some say this was to distinguish street-rodders from the rebellious hot-rodders of yore, but it was more likely reflecting the fact that drag racing and hot rods had diverged, and that rodders now got their kicks from driving modernized early cars or cars that were little more than caricatures of early models. The crazy Fad T rods were massively popular at this time, and usually required huge rear wheels and tyres, the ones in front being so small they resembled motorcycle wheels. In between, there was usually a huge V8 engine and a fibreglass T-bucket – based on the 1923 Ford T – with a shortened Model T

OPPOSITE, LEFT & RIGHT: New disc brakes have been adapted to an older technology in the transversely sprung beam front axle. Note how Rat Fink gets everywhere!

LEFT: BKTOFUN easily translates as 'back to fun' on the licence plate of this Fad T.

pickup bed. Tall windshields, vintage lights, brass radiator grilles and vast quantities of chrome gave these cars a particularly wild appearance.

An exception to the general run of 1970s cars was the California Kid. This was a black 1934 three-window coupé, decorated with flames, that appeared in the TV movie of the same name, starring Martin Sheen, after it had appeared on the cover of *Rod and Custom* magazine. It was built by Pete Chapouris, who restored the bodywork and rebuilt the car with a 1968 Ford 302-ci (4949-cc) V8 engine and C8 automatic transmission. It was named *Hot Rod* magazine's 'Street Rod of the Year' for 1978 when it appeared in the March issue of the magazine.

Production of an unchanged Ford Ranchero continued in 1975, although the Bronco was revised to include a stronger rear axle, reflecting its popularity for off-road use. Later in the year, it was further upgraded when it was given disc brakes on the front axle. Exterior styling remained unchanged on Ford's range of pickups and only minor upgrades were made elsewhere. The range continued as it was with only a minor facelift for the year of America's bicentennial, 1976. The long-running Bronco was designated the U-150 in 1978 and was redesigned to enable it

OPPOSITE: A standard show Fad T, its vintage lights contrasting with the modern V8 engine.

ABOVE: Rodded vans, such as this early hauler, are useful for rod runs, offering plenty of space in which to accomodate life's essentials.

to share standard parts with the F-series trucks and also to change its appearance. Sales more than doubled in the following 12 months, which took Ford into the 1980s along with the further redesigned fleet of F-prefixed trucks.

In 1976 a survey in *Popular Mechanics* magazine found that 53.9 per cent of Ford van owners used their vehicles for recreation

In 1977 Gary Gilmore was executed in a Utah State Prison, the first convict to have been condemned to death in the USA in ten years. In the same year, Chevrolet saw its sales exceed one million a year: after 60 years of truck manufacture, the company had made a total of 21,850,083 trucks. Meanwhile, the LUV models put Chevrolet firmly on the mini-truck map and were to maintain the company's strong position in this sector until

the introduction of the compact Chevrolet S-10 in 1981. The 1977 Chevy LUV was available in two wheelbase lengths, 102.4 and 117.9in (260 and 299cm) and according to the sales brochure for that year, was 'tough enough to be a Chevy'. The LUV was powered by a four-cylinder 80-bhp engine, which according to Environmental Protection Agency (EPA) estimates, returned 34mpg on the highway and 24 in urban use. Numerous options were available, including the Mighty Mike decal package, a rear-step fender, automatic transmission, air conditioning and

an AM/FM radio. Interior trim levels included the more luxurious Mikado package, with a further option of high-backed bucket seats in place of bench.

In the late 1970s Tommy Walsh, Gary Meadors and Bill Burnham formed the Goodguys Rod and Custom Association following a garage-warming party. The organization – originally known as the Danville Dukes – was an informal group without rules, but it is now one of street-rodding's most respected event organizers.

The K30 4x4 one-ton models were added

OPPOSITE: This 1934 Ford two-door sedan has a top-chop so subtle, that it is not immediately obvious.

to the full-size Chevrolet line-up in 1977, and with them came Bonus Cab and Crew Cab models, while the grille was redesigned and power windows were added to the list of available options. The K prefix continued to indicate a Chevrolet 4x4 model, and by 1977 it was possible to buy a GMC K3500 Crew Cab Wideside 4x4 pickup, though the 4x4 option would have added $1,248 to the basic price. Other variations were also available, such as the Desert Fox trim option of 1978, reflecting the popularity of off-road desert racing in the USA. Indy Hauler trucks were also built to mark the GMC company's involvement in the Indy 500, when GMC trucks were made official speedway vehicles during the famous race.

In 1978 the Chevrolet truck chassis was slightly redesigned to make space for a catalytic converter, initially required only in California. There were a number of minor styling upgrades for 1979, including changes to the grille. In 1977 the front end of the Ford Ranchero had been redesigned to incorporate stacked rectangular headlights, while production of the other Ford trucks continued in a similar style as before. The number of options, variations and body types meant that vehicles such as a F-150 Ranger XLT Flareside 4x4 Pickup became possible, XLT being a trim level and Flareside Ford's description of its stepside models. The Plymouth Trail Dusters received a minor facelift for 1977, when the grille was

redesigned to incorporate horizontal bars and vertical signal lights, while the Plymouth badge was shifted from the centre of the grille to the face of the hood. The standard engine was an in-line six-cylinder, although a V8 was an option. Meanwhile, IHC's Scout II remained in production, with few changes beyond a slightly different range of optional V8 engines. The production run of the Scout II would last until 1980, after which time IHC decided to concentrate on heavy trucks. The last years of the Scouts saw them increasingly aimed at the sport utility market, although pickups were also made, including the Scout II Terra Compact Sport Pickup.

Fun with Cars
The ninth annual US Street Rod Nationals, held in Columbus, Ohio, in July 1978, attracted more than 5,000 pre-1941 cars. In the same year, Americans bought an estimated four million pickups. The Ford Bronco was completely restyled and now closely resembled the full-sized Ford pickups, which had also been restyled for this model year. The grille was set higher and featured a rectangular design, the amber lights were set below the headlamps, and a new fender was installed. The types of cab and transmission in 4x2 or 4x4 configurations were retained, as were the F-100, F-150, F-250 and F-350 model designations. Things continued in a similar way for 1979, although the trucks were fitted with rectangular headlights. The Plymouth models were left unchanged for 1978, after the redesign of 1977, but new options were offered in the form of different seats, tinted glass, tilt steering columns and a

CB radio integrated with the AM/FM stereo. New for 1979 was the Plymouth Arrow, a downsized mini-pickup, made by Mitsubishi in Japan for Plymouth, and powered by an in-line four-cylinder engine of 122ci (2000cc) displacement. A Sport package for the same truck was also offered that included bucket seats, extra dashboard gauges, spoked-sport wheels and decals.

Dodge introduced a factory hot-rod truck in 1978, known as the Li'l Red Truck, which followed on from its black-painted Warlock model of 1976. Much of the decade of the 1970s is remembered as the muscle-car era and although it was almost over by 1978, the Li'l Red Truck was a fitting swansong, being the first muscle truck. It was based on the D150 truck, powered by a 360-ci (5899-cc) V8: the prototype had W2 cylinder heads and a Holley four-barrel carburettor, and would run mid-14s out on the quarter-mile strip, where the muscle cars decided who was boss. Eventually, slightly lower performance versions, which would run mid-15s, were offered to the public through Dodge dealers. They were finished in red, trimmed with the 'adventurer' package, with wooden bed details and gold decals. The truck was offered for two consecutive years: in 1978 2,188 were made and in 1979 5,118. The second-year models had dual square headlamps at each side of the grille, whereas the earlier one had single round lights. The later model also featured a catalytic converter as emissions regulations tightened their grip. Three Li'l Red Trucks ran in the infamous Baja 1000 desert race during 1979, in conjunction with Walker Evans, Dodge's noted off-road racer. Two made it to

the finish in La Paz, Mexico, while the third suffered a punctured radiator and was forced to retire.

Late-1970s Hot Rods
The 1980 range of Chevrolet trucks, introduced in the fall of 1979, was large and included two- and four-wheel-drive Fleetside and Stepside models, as well as two- and four-wheel-drive Fleetside Sport and Stepside Sport models; two- and four- wheel-drive crew cab and bonus cab models; two- and four-wheel-drive chassis-cab models for specialist rear bodies, such as wrecker trucks; as well as the C-10 diesel pickup and the heavy-duty BIG-10 pickup. 'Name the job there's a truck here to match,' said Chevrolet. Four trim packages were listed: Standard Custom Deluxe, Scottsdale, Cheyenne and Silverado, the latter being the most luxurious. Some street-rod fashions of the time, inspired by mainstream and other automotive trends, were questioned by more traditional rodders. These included raised white-letter tyres, tops on roadsters, fenders and luggage racks on roadsters, spare wheels on Hiboys, wide wire wheels, extra spotlights, trailers, van-type murals, low-profile tyres, unchopped roofs and even fenders! By now, the 1980s were just around the corner and times were changing fast.

As the 1980s decade began, shops specializing in big street rods, that advertised in rodding magazines, built top-quality cars and supplied components, included Pete and Jake's of Temple City, California; Total Performance Inc of Wallingford, Connecticut; The Deuce Factory of Santa Ana, California; The Florida Rodshop of Palm Harbor, Florida; and Mr Roadster of Baltimore, Ohio. In January 1980, Model A chassis dating from 1928–31, were available from Specialty Cars of Artesia, California; The Florida Rodshop of Palm Harbor, Florida; Bill's Rod and Custom of Springfeld, Ohio; Paul's Street Rod Parts of Placentia, California; TCI Engineering of Ontario, California; Hamilton Automotive Industries of Van Nuys, California; Progressive Automotive of Baltimore, Ohio; and Total Perfomance Inc of Wallingford Connecticut. The 1932 Ford chassis was available from Florida Rodshop of Palm Harbor, Florida; Bill's Rod and Custom of Springfeld, Ohio; Paul's Street Rod Parts of Placentia, California; TCI Engineering of Ontario, California; Hamilton Automotive Industries of Van Nuys, California; Progressive Automotive of Baltimore, Ohio; Total Performance Inc of Wallingford, Connecticut; The Deuce Factory of Santa Ana,

LEFT: Flames and early Ford sheetmetal never go out of style.

OPPOSITE:
While flame decoration is timeless, modern alloy wheels place this rod very much in the present.

California; and the Beverly Hills Street Rod Shop of Van Nuys, California. The 1933–34 Ford chassis was available from Specialized Auto Components of Anaheim, California, and Progressive Automotive of Baltimore, Ohio. Chassis for various models of Model T Ford were available from Specialty Cars of Artesia, California; Florida Rodshop of Palm Harbor, Florida; Hamilton Automotive Industries of Van Nuys, California; and Total Performance Inc of Wallingford, Connecticut.

During the 1980s GMC was to adopt a new strategy and stop manufacturing heavy-duty trucks, preferring to concentrate on the booming medium- and light-duty markets. The Silverado models were given rectangular headlights, but the major changes came in 1981. GMC made only cosmetic changes to its range of trucks as the company entered the 1980s, although the square-patterned ice-cube-tray radiator grille remained. An extra-cost option that demonstrated the direction in which auto-styling was heading, was the dual

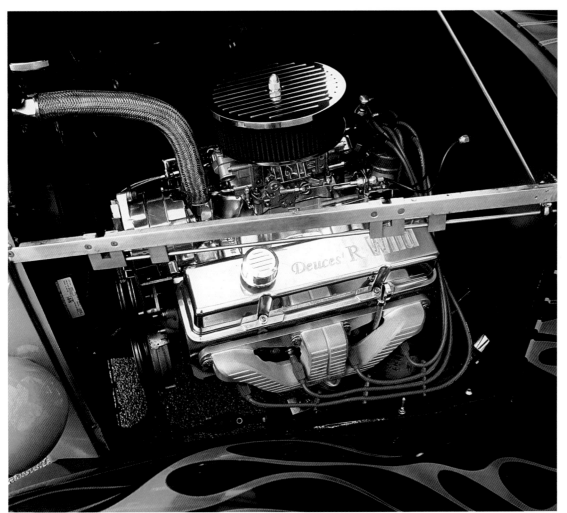

OPPOSITE: The subtle appearance belies the work
required to hide components, such as tail lights,
so that a smooth finish can be achieved.

LEFT: Attention to detail is equally evident under
the hood.

stacked rectangular headlamps on either side
of the grille, rather than the single circular
ones that were fitted as standard. The Half-
Ton models retained an in-line six-cylinder
engine as standard, while the other base
models had a V8 engine as standard. This
programme of minor upgrades continued into
the 1981 models: for example, detail
upgrades were made to the transmission of
the 4x4 variants and the front sheetmetal of
both Jimmys and pickups was redesigned to
make it more aerodynamic and so improve
fuel efficiency.

Big car shows were held indoors during
the 1980s, such as the World of Wheels, held
at the Los Angeles Convention Center. In
January 1980, the 18th annual event,
sanctioned by the International Show Car
Association (ISCA), featured custom cars,
lowriders, vans, motorcycles, pickups, off-
road vehicles, race cars and drag boats,
alongside the street rods. Show cars of note
included Farrah Fawcett-Majors's Chevrolet
Corvette and the Pool Hustler, the latter being
a surprising hybrid of a single-seat race car
and a pool table, and was about as far from a
street-driven hot rod as it was possible to be.
At the other end of the spectrum, later in the
year, was the 6th annual Yesteryear Drags,
Rod Run and Swap Meet, promoted by Street
Rods Unlimited at Orange County Raceway.

OPPOSITE & ABOVE: Two contrasting approaches to rodding Model A five-window coupés.

The event was open to pre-1958 vehicles and the emphasis was on driving old iron. The trend towards driving soon began to catch on again, when Rollin' Rods of South Jersey promoted the 1st Annual Old-Time Drags and Rod Run at Raceway Park in Englishtown, New Jersey. By 1981, the World of Wheels show exhibits included the Pizza Wagon and Pinball Wizard. These rods were extreme versions of the C-Cab-style Model T van and Fad T respectively, with heavily moulded bodywork, blown V8 engine, and high-tech big and little wheel and tyre combinations. As the name of the latter suggests, it incorporated a pinball machine into the rear bodywork: both machines, while they were creative, had little in common with street-driven cars. The same people, Promotions Inc, staged other

ISCA World of Wheels events, including one in Boston that also featured the Pinball Wizard with the Red Baron, another themed rod. Again, this was a T-based creation that included a Model T grille, straight-six engine with upturned chromed headers, and a cab made from a larger-than-life German *pickelhaube* helmet. The Cavalcade of Customs for 1981, at the Cincinnati Convention Center, included the Charlie's Angels Van and one of the General Lee 1969 Dodge Chargers, that had been built for the TV series, The Dukes of Hazzard.

With the benefit of hindsight, it seems that the 1980s began in a low-key kind of way: the Moscow Olympic Games were shunned by several countries, including the USA, that was opposed to Russia's military action in Afghanistan. Ongoing at the time was a presidential race that involved the Republican Ronald Reagan and Democrat Jimmy Carter. Reagan went on to win the race, becoming the USA's 40th president, and soon after survived an assassination attempt. The Philadelphia Phillies won their first World Series baseball tournament in 98 years, while the arrival of a new chairman, Lee Iacocca, at Chrysler, made exciting news in automotive circles. Ford advertised its F-100 as the 'first new truck of the eighties' and produced redesigned models, including a number of 'custom' paint options with contrasting panels. The model designations remained unchanged, so it was still possible to buy a Ford half-ton F-150 Custom Flareside 4x4 Pickup. The Ford 4x4 models now featured a new front suspension system, known as the Twin-Traction Beam independent suspension, while in the same year, the Ranchero pickup was dropped from the Ford range. Sales of early-1980s models generally declined, because of the poor state of the US economy. Ford continued to sell its compact Mazda-built Courier pickups, and turned some of its attention to more fuel-efficient vehicles. The styling of the F-series trucks remained the same, although minor upgrades included the removal of the word Ford from the front edge of the hood, when the famous blue oval in the centre of the grille was substituted. In March 1982, the downsized Ranger pickup made its

ABOVE LEFT: This 1940 Ford Woody is a stylish and practical street rod.

ABOVE: An early pickup makes a great street rod.

OPPOSITE: This 1940 Ford coupé has a particularly curvaceous body.

debut with styling similar to that of the F-100; by now it had become a model in its own right, rather than a trim option of an Effie. The Bronco II made its debut only a year later, and sold at two-and-a-half times its previous rate.

In February 1981, a sign that street rods were making the transition to Main Street from time to time, was the news that George Barris, self-proclaimed 'king of the kustomizers' and Dick Dean had built the Geoffreymobile double-decker, as a promotional vehicle for the Toys R Us chain of stores. The Geoffreymobile, that supposedly ran on potato chips, was the subject of a storybook, depicted as a fantasy car owned by a family of giraffes. In reality,

it used rather a lot of Fad T street-rod styling, including a C-cab and a Model T-style grille. It was a front-wheel-drive machine, with a Dick Dean-engineered VW transaxle coupled with a Ford Taunus V4 engine for power, and steered by a Saab set-up.

An indication of the scale of the industry that had grown up around building street rods, was the fact that in November 1981, *Rod Action* magazine carried advertisements for Super Bell Axle Co, Total Performance

OPPOSITE, ABOVE & LEFT: Larry Sterkel's Colorado-based 1935 closed-cab Ford pickup relies on standard-type steelwork, meticulous attention to detail in its assembly, and flawless Porsche-red paintwork.

LEFT: A 1980s take on the perennial favourite, the chopped 1932 three-window coupé.

OPPOSITE: This fully-fendered Model T-based Woody is an unusual but neat street rod.

Inc, Gibbon Fiberglass Reproductions Inc, Street Rod Equipment, Pete and Jake's, Rodtin Interior Products, The Deuce Factory, Vintage Auto Parts Inc, Brizio Street Rods, MAS Racing Products, Auto America, Specialty Cars, Reliable Auto Accessories, TCI Engineering, Poli Form Industries, Bird Automotive, Walker Radiator Works, Vintage Chassis Works, Chassis Engineering, Al's Antique Autoparts, Specialized Auto Components, Vintage Air, Florida Rod Shop Inc, The Khrome Shoppe, A1 Fiberglass, Classic Instruments Inc, Butch's Rod Shop, Rootlieb Inc, Posies, Competition Cams and Bill's Rod and Custom. A year later, *Hot Rod*, now considerably more mainstream, carried advertisements for Chevrolet, AC-Delco, Panasonic, Isky Cams, B&M, Midas, Racing Unlimited Inc, American Motors Corporation, Goodyear, Pontiac, Accel, Trans American Automotive, Ford Ranger pickups, Discount Parts and Tires, Earl's Performance Products, Southern Performance Specialty, Summit Racing, GMC trucks, as well as lifestyle ads for cigarettes and whisky; Winston, Kool, Salem Lights, Camel, Marlboro and Seagram's 7. Pre-1948 cars were thin on the ground, where it came to editorial coverage, represented only by a 1931 Ford, 1937 Plymouth, 1938 Ford and by a retrospective on the Stone, Woods and Cook Willys gassers.

The key trophy at the annual Oakland

Roadster Show is the one awarded for 'America's Most Beautiful Roadster', which in 1982 went to Jamie Musselman's 1933 Ford. This roadster had been built by Boyd Coddington, who had given a modern and high-tech twist to a traditional hot-rod roadster. It featured a Chevy V8 and had a smooth appearance, enhanced by billet-alloy wheels. Later in the year, *Hot Rod* built a 'repro rod' from new parts ordered over the telephone. It was a Deuce Highboy, powered by a blown Buick V6. This showed the comprehensiveness of the selection of specialist street-rod components now available.

By this time, former dry-lakes racer, Stan Betz, had been in business for more than two decades as the proprietor of Betz Speed and

ABOVE: A fenderless 1932 roadster with flames.

ABOVE LEFT: A chopped 1934 coupé, similarly treated.

LEFT: A tough-looking chopped 1932 coupé.

OPPOSITE: Street rod meets 4x4: the classic 1950s Chevy pickup on a Chevy Blazer chassis and running gear.

Color in Orange, Californa, and had built an unusual rod in the shape of a 1939 American Austin Bantam roadster, even though they were mostly used as the bases of drag cars. Powered by a 1962 in-line four-cylinder Chevrolet engine, the diminutive rod had been work in progress for 17 years, but

OPPOSITE: This fenderless 1932 roadster street rod is a timeless classic.

LEFT: Modified classic trucks, such as this F-100, possess many street-rod influences.

emerged in a form that was completely at home in the early-1980s. Meanwhile, back on Main Street, new from GMC for 1982 were the S-15 model trucks, on which work had begun in 1978, as a response to the increasing popularity of the smaller-sized imported trucks, known as Minis, such as the Chevy LUV, which was really an Isuzu with Chevrolet badges. The S-15 was similar in size to the LUV and by 1983 4x4 and extended-cab models were also available. The downsized GMC four-wheel-drive Jimmy was based around the S-15, and featured a tailgate and two doors on a 100.5-in (255-cm) wheelbase. The Chevrolet S-10 of 1982 was a compact that replaced the Chevy LUV and was available in two- and later four-wheel-drive. Meanwhile, Dodge had shifted production to more aerodynamic pickups and a downsized model, the front-wheel-drive Rampage, a sport truck. Trucks such as the Chevy LUV fuelled the impetus for the mini-trucking fad, that were somewhere between custom vans and street rods. Over the course of the next decade, the market in pickup trucks would shift considerably, and sport trucks and sport utilities were to become mainstream America's major auto purchases, the compact Chevrolet S-10 being at the forefront of this trend.

During 1983 the US Marines suffered

LEFT: This modified 1954 Chevrolet pickup is a great truck to drive.

BELOW LEFT & BELOW: The late-1960s Chevrolet pickup is considered a classic truck, rather than a rod, but the street-rod influences are obvious.

OPPOSITE: Replica of the ZZ Top Eliminator, a 1934 Ford coupé street rod.

more than 200 fatalities, when their Beirut base was bombed, but later in the same month soldiers from the same outfit were tasked with the controversial invasion of Grenada, in the effort to preserve its democracy. The January 1983 issue of *Hot Rod* featured advertisements for the 1983 Dodge Charger, Performance Automotive Wholesale, Midwest Auto Specialties, Mitsubishi pickups, Salem cigarettes, Marlboro cigarettes, Kool Filter kings,

OPPOSITE: Driving a 1934 Ford coupé resto rod on wide wire wheels, is a great way to enjoy rod-runs.

ABOVE: A dragster, based on a 1929 Model A sedan delivery.

Winston cigarettes, Summit Racing Equipment, Racing Unlimited Inc, Datsun 4x4 pickups and Camel cigarettes. How often the pre-1948 'rule' had been broken is illustrated by the list of included features: Chevy street machines and muscle cars, Tommy Ivo's four-engined 1961 dragster, wiring how-tos, a Buick V8-powered MGB sports car, an axle-narrowing how-to, a 1936 Ford Kustom, a 1982 Ford Ranger stepside pickup, the magazine's own project, a 1982 Camaro IMSA racer, a 1927 Model T dragster, a 1979 Chevrolet Stepside pickup, and the 1983 Japanese production bikes, that aimed for tens on the dragstrip, straight off the showroom floor. Street rods were only to be seen in a two-page spread on a pair of Chevrolet rods, a spread on a 1932 Ford Victoria street rod, and in Gray Baskerville's column, writing about his own basket case of a 1932 Roadster, originally built in the early 1960s by Paul Horning. In the February 1983 edition of *Popular Hot-Rodding* magazine, there were no feature cars that

OPPOSITE: Rumble seats turn two-seater roadsters into family rods.

ABOVE: A 1937 Ford-based Woody.

ABOVE RIGHT: Another Ford-based Woody, this time from 1940.

RIGHT: Swap meets are a vital source of street-rod parts.

PAGE 142: This chopped 1934 coupé has plenty of dragstrip attitude.

PAGE 143: The blower hints at what is hidden under the sheetmetal of this 1932 Ford.

fitted the generally accepted definition of a hot rod, its pages being full of muscle cars, a classic F-100 pickup and a pro-street Datsun pickup. In fact, the only pre-1948 car featured was a 454 Chevy-powered 1927 T dragster, that ran the quarter in 8.50 seconds at 155mph (249km/h).

Like Milner's yellow coupé of the 1970s, another street rod appeared in the early 1980s that became world-famous and gave street-rodding a massive boost. It was the Eliminator, built for Billy Gibbons of the ZZ Top rock band. It was a 1933 steel three-window Ford coupé. The car was built by Jake Jacobs, who began with the original Ford chassis and strengthened it. This was to allow it to accept a 350-ci (5735-cc) Chevy V8 and GM automatic three-speed transmission. The engine benefits from a

single 650-cfm, four-barrel Holley carburettor and custom headers. The front axle is a transversely-sprung unit from Bell, with Mustang disc brakes, while the rear axle has 1957 Ford 9-in (23-cm) drum brakes on leaf springs. The ride is dampened by a set of Spax dampers, while the coupé's roof was chopped 3in (8cm), and finally cleaned up by Steve Davis and Don 'Buffy' Thelan.

In the typical style of the 1980s, the car was fitted with 15in (38cm) diameter Centerline Wheels, fitted with radial BF Goodrich tyres – 185 sections at the front and 255 at the rear to give the slightly nose-down appearance. The coupé was painted red with a few additional graphics representing the ZZ Top logo. The car's name was also the title of the band's 1983 album, and the car soon became famous worldwide after appearing in the band's music videos, accompanied by long-legged ladies. Every so often, a band hits a groove mid-career and produces an album that is just right for its time. The Eliminator album was one such record: radio stations played 'Legs' and 'Sharp Dressed Man' until the grooves all but disappeared, while fans simply ate up the songs, the videos and the 1933 coupé!

As the content of *Hot Rod* magazine suggests, pickups were becoming increasingly important in enthusiast circles at this time. New from Ford for 1984 was the

RIGHT: Flame decoration and alloy wheels make this English Ford a great rod.

OPPOSITE: A street-legal, chopped 1932 Ford coupé, preparing for a run on the dragstrip.

OPPOSITE: Old and new are seamlessly combined in this rodded 1932 closed-cab pickup truck.

ABOVE: The 1932 Tudor Sedan: the two-door model was Ford's most popular Deuce.

ABOVE RIGHT: A tough-looking version of the 1941 Willys pickup gasser.

RIGHT: A nice example of the perennially popular 1932 Ford roadster.

downsized Bronco II sport utility, designed along similar lines as the compact Ranger pickup. The F-100 was discontinued and the F-150 became the base model in a range that still included the F-250 and F-350 pickups, and by the middle of the decade the Ranger and Bronco II were established in Ford's range of light-duty trucks, along with the full-sized F-150, F-250 and F-350 models. For 1984, the limited-edition GMC Indy Hauler pickup was unveiled to celebrate the Indy 500 motor race. It was based on an S-15 extended-cab model, and was one of numerous options offered that year. The full-sized GMC trucks continued into the mid-1980s, with the same general appearance as before, although the programme of sequential upgrades continued. Suspension and engine were two of the areas where refinements were made. Pickups in both wideside and fenderside variants continued to be manufactured and, as a result of increasing awareness of fuel economy, diesel options were introduced into the range.

The NSRA Nationals had continued into the new decade with events held in Memphis, Tennessee in 1980; Columbus, Ohio in 1981; St Paul, Minnesota in 1982; Oklahoma City, Oklahoma in 1983; Columbus, Ohio in 1984; St Paul, Minnesota in 1985; Oklahoma City, Oklahoma in 1986; Columbus, Ohio in 1987; Louisville, Kentucky in 1988 and St Paul, Minnesota in 1989. The 1980s saw a surge of interest, as new fashions emerged, including graphics, billet-aluminium components facilitated by the arrival of the CNC machine, increasing numbers of reproduction parts, especially good-quality fibreglass bodies, while a wider selection of custom wheels became increasingly available. Street-rodding, ever evolving, incorporated these trends, that also found acceptance with the builders of other modified vehicles, especially in the

realm of pickups. The 1980s also saw awakening feelings of nostalgia for rods of the past, which, metaphorically-speaking, had gone in the opposite direction from the smoothed-out, billet-wheeled, high-tech rods presently being produced.

ABOVE: Alloy wheels give this chopped-top sedan delivery a modern look.

ABOVE RIGHT: WD PEKR (Woodpecker) is a 1936 Ford Woody.

RIGHT: This closed-cab 1932 Ford pickup sits low on chromed steel wheels with hubcaps.

OPPOSITE: Very few 1932 Ford sedan deliveries were manufactured: this is a modern rod version.

CHAPTER EIGHT
THE NINETIES & BEYOND:
STREET RODS ON MAIN STREET

The issue of *Hot Rod* magazine for August 1990 contained features on a rodded 1936 coupé, a 1940 Sedan Delivery, and little else in the way of pre-1948 cars, though some of the modified classic 1950s pickups bore witness to the rising popularity of classic American pickups and the pro-street look, while advertisements indicated the popularity of pickups in general. A year later, and it was a similar story, as street machines, muscle cars and pro-streeters filled most of the editorial pages, leaving street rods to compete for space. A 1933 and 1940 Ford did manage to make it, however, as did coverage of the Hot Rod Supernationals, while Gray Baskerville detailed a new starter kit for a repro 1932 Ford roadster rod, made by California Street Rods. Despite the trend apparent at *Hot Rod* magazine, street-rodding was alive and well: it was just that it was chronicled in greater depth in magazines such as *Street Rodder*. By 1991, mini-trucks and sport trucks were big news; the S-10 and C-series pickups, and their respective Blazer

RIGHT: A 1940 Ford pickup in Reno, Nevada.

OPPOSITE: Out on the streets in Reno, during a rod-run on a Hot August Night event..

and Suburban sport-utility derivatives being of equal importance in the Chevrolet model line-up. The 1990s generation of the C- and K-series trucks were available with petrol and diesel engines, short- and long-load boxes, regular and extended cabs, and in three levels of trim – Cheyenne, Scottsdale and Silverado. There was a similar degree of

OPPOSITE: The stance and the modern wheels indicate a modern version of the 1934 coupé rod.

ABOVE & RIGHT: The 1932 Ford roadster is probably the most popular of the early Fords. V8s are traditionally used as hot-rod engines.

choice for purchasers of the S-10 compact pickup, with the exception of the diesel-powered variant. The varying trim levels were referred to as Standard and Tahoe, and there was an additional Baja off-road trim package for 4x4 models. The S-10 Blazer came in two- or four-door models, with choice of 4x2 and 4x4 transmissions, and featured an Electronic Fuel Injection (EFI) V6 engine, while the trim levels offered were the same as for the S-10. The full-sized Blazer was powered by a V8 petrol or diesel engine, with a choice of Scottsdale or Silverado trim and either two- or four-wheel-drive. The APV (All Purpose Vehicle) was a new addition to the Chevrolet light truck

range and also available were the Astro passenger van, the Lumina APV and the Sportvan. A spectacular Sport Truck from Chevrolet completed the 1991 range, although it had originally been introduced in 1989, being a truck reminiscent of the muscle-car era of the 1970s. This was the 454 SS – a 454ci (7440cc) V8- powered C1500 Fleetside pickup, finished in Onyx Black. Meanwhile, away from home, there was massive American involvement, helped by coalition forces, in the 1991 Gulf War against Iraq.

By 1993 the 454 SS Chevrolet truck was facing competition from Ford in the shape of the Ford F-150 Lightning, powered by Ford's smaller-displacement 351-ci (5752-cc) V8, albeit in a tuned form. Comparison tests of the time, made in *Automotive* magazine, gave the Ford the lead in terms of all-round use, but the 454 SS Chevrolet was beyond

ABOVE: *A Willys gasser in Reno, Nevada.*

OPPOSITE: *Such is the extent of the components supply chain, that it is possible to buy roadster tops for chopped windshields.*

doubt the leader in muscle-truck terms. The Ford line-up for the early 1990s was comprehensive and based around three models: the F-150, F-250 and F-350, with maximum gross vehicle weights of 6,250, 8,600 and 11,000lb (2835, 3900 and 4990kg) respectively, while there were correspondingly increasing payloads of 2,145, 3,915 and 5,890lb (973, 1776 and. 2672kg). There was a choice of four body styles: Regular Cab, Super Cab, Crew Cab and Flareside, and three trim levels: S, XL and XLT, which accounts for 36 different variants before the engine options are even considered. There were six different engines, ranging from the standard 4.9-litre in-line six

through a 5.0-litre V8, a 5.8-litre V8, a 7.3-litre indirect-injection diesel V8, a 7.3-litre indirect-injection turbo-diesel V8 to a 7.5-litre V8. This brought the number of F-series variants to 216 without the various transmissions. There were four possibilities,

LEFT: Every curve of the Deuce is perfect.

BELOW LEFT: Modern street rods are built from the chassis up.

BELOW: Modern street-rod shops are kept clinically clean.

OPPOSITE: The licence plate, 1FINE39 says it all.

which included both manual and autoboxes, and increased the number of F-series variants to 864. Competition with Chevrolet dictated that such a range be available to suit every customer's requirements, and Chevrolet offered a similar choice of body styles, engine options and transmissions. New for 1994 were air bags on the driver's side in F-150 and F-250 models, side-door impact bars as stock across the range, and a brake shift interlock system as standard on all autobox models.

While Chevrolet and Ford were slugging it out between themselves in the full-sized truck class, the mini-van trend was gaining popularity; on offer to American buyers in 1993 were the Chevrolet Astro, Ford Aerostar, Pontiac Tran Sport and Plymouth Voyager, as well as Mazda and Toyota models, while in the compact truck market, Ford's Ranger Flareside was creating a stir. Half-way through the model year, Ford introduced the Ford Ranger Flareside Splash, a sport version of the Ranger pickup. It was euphemistically described as the truck for the 'under-30 crowd' and was inspired by the trend towards 'personal use' pickups in states such as California. The Splash featured a restyled pickup box that followed the stylized lines of the new Ranger: indeed the cab-forward sheetmetal was 1993 Ranger, though it more than hinted at stepside styling. The Flareside was powered by a V6 engine and had a five-speed manual transmission. Its overall appearance was enhanced by a single-colour paint scheme, and included colour-keyed fenders, offset with chrome wheels and coloured graphics.

The concept of the compact truck had been totally accepted by the mid 1990s, its perceived advantages being fuel economy, versatility, practicality and a rugged quality lacking in cars. The manufacturers were aware of its growing popularity and in 1994 the American big three, Ford, Dodge and General Motors' Chevrolet and GMC, all offered compact pickups – the Ranger, Ram 50 and S-Series respectively. The Ram 50

OPPOSITE, LEFT & BELOW: This fat-fendered late-1930s Chevrolet rod features the sort of decoration popular in the 1990s.

was a rebadged Mitsubishi, while at least six importers also offered trucks. The distinction between American manufacturers and importers was becoming blurred, however, as around 74 per cent of the Isuzu compact

OPPOSITE: A 1990s-style Chevrolet truck rod.

ABOVE: A fenderless Deuce roadster with classic paint job.

ABOVE RIGHT: A completely different take on the flame-decorated Deuce roadster concept.

RIGHT: The smoothed-out phaeton is yet another take on the open-topped Deuce.

OPPOSITE, ABOVE & RIGHT: Hellrod is a 1932 Tudor Sedan, heavily influenced by the dragstrip.

PAGE 164: A lowriding 1941 Willys coupé, with a blown engine.

PAGE 165: A Model A Ford roadster pickup, with modern whitewall tyres.

trucks sold in the USA in 1993 and 1994 were built at the company's plant in Lafayette, Indiana. For 1994 Mazda started to manufacture its B4000-series trucks, variants of the Ford Ranger, in the USA. Also new for 1994 were the completely redesigned GMC S-series trucks, known as the GMC Sonoma, while the Chevrolet retained the S-10 designation and was available in various trim levels in both 4x2 and 4x4 forms.

There was also a major development for 1994 in the full-sized truck, when Dodge introduced a new-model Ram, more than 20 years after its previous one first appeared. The full-size market was at that time divided

almost exclusively between Ford and Chevrolet, but the Dodge was to change this division of the market share. The styling of the Ram had clearly been influenced by the 18-wheeler big rigs, but it combined modern aerodynamic styling with the distinctive look of vintage trucks. In designing the truck, Chysler's designers were trying to leap-frog ahead of the established Chevy and Ford styling, well aware that anyone buying its truck would first have to be tempted away from these two marques. The new Dodge Ram, made in Warren, Michigan, was offered with a choice of V6, V8 and V10 gasoline or Cummins turbo-diesel engines. Two- and four-wheel-drive transmissions were also available and the truck was offered in three series, half-ton 1500, three-quarter-ton 2500

ABOVE & OPPOSITE: Chuck Hill's 1929 Model A Ford roadster pickup, powered by a 1967 289-ci (4736-cc) Ford V8, has an automatic gearbox, disc brakes and American Racing Equipment alloy wheels.

and one-ton 3500: the 318ci (5211cc) V8 half-tonner had a four-speed autobox that would turn a quarter-mile in 17 seconds. Another development for 1994 was the running of the first NASCAR Truck exhibition race at the Mesa Marin Raceway in Bakersfield, California. NASCAR racing had long been a leading form of autosport in America, but had been restricted to cars. The exhibition race for trucks in 1994 only had four trucks on the grid, but by 1997 truck-racing had become almost as big as the car series. Trucks decked out in the decals of national corporate sponsors represented numerous truck manufacturers, including Chevrolet, Dodge and Ford.

In 1994 the 25th-anniversary NSRA Nationals took place, and the following year the 26th was held in Syracuse, New York. By now, all SCTA racing, with the exception of Bonneville, was taking place at El Mirage in the Mojave Desert of California. The famous Muroc Dry Lake venue is now Edwards Air Force Base, and is the site of NASA space-shuttle landings. Dry-lakes racing ended there in 1938 in the run-up to the Second World War, and was not permitted for almost half a century until 1996, when the SCTA was able to organize a Muroc reunion.

Edwards Air Force Base is located on the borders of Kern County and Los Angeles County, California, in the Antelope Valley,

7 miles (11km) east of Rosamond. An airbase since 1933, Edwards has long been a home for flight research and testing and has subsequently been involved in many important and daring research flights. Originally known as the Muroc Army Air Field, the base was renamed in 1950 in memory of test pilot Glen Edwards, who

died while testing the Northrop YB-49. The base is strategically situated adjacent to Rogers Lake, a desert salt pan, its hard playa surface providing a natural extension to the base's runways. This large landing area, combined with a splendid year-round climate, makes it an excellent site for flight-testing. Designated an Air Force Flight Test

Centre (AFFTC), Edwards is home to the United States Air Force Test Pilot School and NASA's Dryden Flight Research Centre. Almost every United States military aircraft since the 1950s has been at least partially tested there. Appropriate in a place where cars have broken records on the salt, notable occurrences at Edwards include Chuck

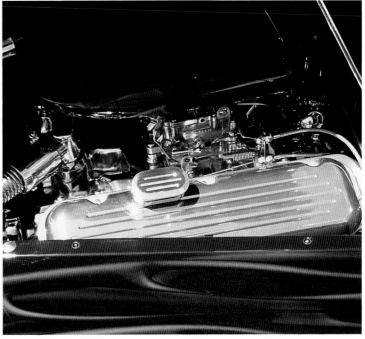

Yeager's famous flight, when he broke the sound barrier in a Bell X-1. This was followed by test flights of the North American X-15, the first landings of the Space Shuttle, the 1986 around-the-world flight of the Scaled Composites Voyager, and was where the concept of Murphy's Law

OPPOSITE: A 1934 roadster with billet-aluminium wheels. Billet components became popular following the advent of the CNC milling machine.

ABOVE & ABOVE RIGHT: A 1934 coupé with billet-aluminium engine components, highly-modified in the 1990s.

originated. Murphy's Law (also known as Finagle's Law or Sod's Law) is a supposed law of nature, humorously expressed in the saying that anything that can go wrong will go wrong. Murphy was Major Edward A Murphy Junior, a development engineer who for a brief time worked on US rocket sled experiments in 1949. His law can quite easily be applied to hot-rodding.

Compact trucks that came from the major domestic US manufacturers in 1997, included the updated Ford Ranger, the Dodge Ram-styled Dakota SLT and the Ford Ranger. This latter had been the top-selling compact truck in the USA for the past decade: for 1998 the model's wheelbase was

extended by 3.6in (9cm) to increase legroom, seat travel and space behind the seats. The available engines, both base model in-line four and optional V6, received slight increases in horsepower. The full-sized Ford pickups, the F-series, celebrated their 50th anniversary in 1998. When advertising the new F-series, Ford was able to say that 'about the only thing it has in common with the typical 50-year old, is the spare tire'. Based on consumer reports, taken after three months, in a survey of Ford and competitive

models designed and built in North America, Ford could claim its trucks were better-built and better-selling than any of its rivals.

By the mid 1990s, the Japanese Toyota company had also constructed a factory within the USA, in Fremont, California, and announced that its new compact pickup truck for 1995 would be built there. The Tacoma was a refined version of its earlier truck and was available in both two- and four-wheel-drive forms, as well as in standard cab and XtraCab forms. XtraCabs are extended

pickup cabs with an area that can have a second row of seats or a secure storage space (various names were given to the type by different manufacturers during the 1990s). The concept had already been realized in the crew cab, that had been popular for decades, and offered a cab with more space without reducing the overall size of the load bed, as was the case with the crew cab, and without extending the truck's wheelbase.

By now, industries supplying speed and custom parts were thriving, producing every kind of street-rodding component imaginable: it was now possible to build

ABOVE: Jimmy Shine's pickup was a ground-breaking retro machine, built after the Millennium.

OPPOSITE: Shine's truck uses an Edelbrock-equipped flathead Ford V8 engine.

PAGE 174: This Deuce roadster uses traditional components but is assembled with modern flair.

PAGE 175: A modern interpretation of the Deuce roadster, with hints of resto rod.

LEFT: *Street-rod influences on this factory-built Plymouth Prowler are obvious.*

OPPOSITE: *This subtle Model A roadster pickup offers a classy ride.*

complete street rods using newly-made reproduction parts, including frames, body panels and engine blocks. For those able to afford it, it was possible to commission a name-built, one-of-a-kind hot rod. By now, hot-rodding had inadvertently found mainstream acceptance, especially with the arrival of the Plymouth Prowler and Chrysler PT Cruiser. Contemporary street-rod styling, similar to that of Boyd Coddington and Bob Larivee's Cosmic Coupé, based on a 1933 coupé with a Mitsubishi Eclipse engine, was much in evidence in some of the most unusual factory-built cars. Chrysler claimed tthe Prowler was Plymouth's tribute to 'a truly original American art form', namely the street rod, and remarked that 'Its odyssey from design idea to concept car to production vehicle is our salute to the spirited, creative passions of those who have made such enduring machines, and re-affirmation of why Chrysler Corporation and its employees design, engineer and manufacture great cars and great trucks in the first place'. The Plymouth Prowler's styling is unashamedly hot-rod; even its cast-aluminium 'big and little' wheels evoke the street rod, its 17-in front and 20-in rears being fitted with P225/45HR17 and P295/40HR20 Goodyear Extended Mobility (EMT) tyres, with run-flat capability and low tyre pressure sensors respectively, while the huge AutoMeter

OPPOSITE: This closed-cab Model A pickup is about as low as it can go.

RIGHT: Pickups, such as this 1951 Ford F-1, are often lowered as part of a restyle.

tachometer has a strapped-on look. The seating position is sporty, and the Prowler has a 250-hp version of the 3.5-litre high-output SOHC 24-valve aluminum V6 engine offering the expected sporting performance. Production of the 113-in (287-cm) wheelbase Prowler began in early 1997 at Chrysler's Conner Avenue Assembly Plant in Detroit. First-year production was projected at 3,000 vehicles and the car was set to be phased out after four years, although production was extended.

The Prowler is made of a high-strength aluminium alloy, as used in airplanes and boats, allowing it to resist degradation, noise, and oxidation. More than 900lb (408kg) of the 2,780-lb (1261-kg) roadster is aluminium, including body, chassis and a number of the suspension components. A new process provided the same body stiffness as a steel car, and careful design allowed for a similar level of safety. Chrysler chose to use rivet bonding, in which a shank of metal is driven into two sheets of aluminium, with epoxy adhesive applied for extra strength: the company estimates that body stiffness increased by 40 per cent using this method. The magnesium instrument panel, which combines more than 20 stamped and plastic components in a single casting, was 8lb (3.6kg) lighter than a

conventional one, while an aluminium seat saved another 7lb, and composite brake rotors yet another 15lb (7kg) of weight. Several aluminium drive-line components not only reduced weight but also vibration. The front and rear suspension assemblies were multi-link systems, and the front was a double wishbone set-up, with upper and lower control arms. The front spring shock assemblies were similar to those used on Indy cars, using a pushrod rocker. The rear suspension used a lower control arm and a three-bar-link upper configuration. The control arms, rocker arms and knuckles (both front and rear) were made using aluminium that was pressurized into a die, similar to

plastic injection moulding. This process, semi-solid-forming, is stronger than traditional casting with less of a tendency to weaken over time. The acceptance of the Prowler by hot-rodders was more than apparent when one was put on display at an event staged by the Goodguys Rod and Custom Association.

The PT Cruiser was another street rod-inspired production car from Chrysler, while the North American PT Cruisers came with a single 2.4-litre engine used in base minivans; it provided sufficient rather than thrilling power. Concept vehicles, such as the Plymouth Pronto, were used to explore the feasibility of different designs. All PT

Cruisers are built in Toluca, USA, and Graz, Austria. The PT Cruiser collected awards such as *Car and Driver*'s Ten Best, the North American Auto Show's Car of the Year and *Motor Trend*'s Car of the Year. The early Pronto concept cars were heavily based on the Neon's floorpan and mechanicals, but as the Pronto evolved into the PT, Chrysler used a beam axle and Watts linkage.

Into a New Century

As the 1990s gave way to the 21st century, museums became repositories of hot-rod history. The Petersen Automotive Museum in Los Angeles and Darryl Starbird's National Rod & Custom Car Hall of Fame Museum in

ABOVE LEFT: A modern version of a 1932 roadster rod.

ABOVE: A rodded 1956 Ford F-100.

OPPOSITE: Rod runs are popular part of street-rodding.

PAGE 182: A contemporary incarnation of a 1940 Ford pickup.

PAGE 183: The flame treatment suits flat-fendered Fords, just as it does the earlier models.

Tulsa, Oklahoma, have preserved a substantial part of the history of the movement, while the trend towards 1940s hot rods and rat rods suggests that hot-rodding will be with us for some time to come, even though there will be legislative issues to be overcome. Emissions laws are one aspect of this, and what 21st-century street rods exactly are is a question yet to be answered. The early years of the 21st century saw the return of 1970s trends, while remakes of TV shows and movies saw the reinvention of popular cars. *Gone in Sixty Seconds*, premiered in 2000, retells the tale of a car thief who stole 50 cars, including a classic Mustang, while a film recently appeared based on Starsky and Hutch, a TV series originally from the 1970s, in which the real star was Starsky's red-and-white Ford Torino. *Hot Rod* magazine featured a behind-the-scenes feature on the recreation of the

ABOVE: Smooth lines, billet wheels, and interesting graphics, date this as a 1990s street rod.

OPPOSITE: This 1937 Chevrolet has received similar treatment.

LEFT: The 1932 Ford rod retains legions of fans.

OPPOSITE: A modern version of the Model A sedan rod.

PAGE 188: Larger payload-versions of vintage trucks, especially the Cab-Over-Engine (COE) models, have become increasingly popular as a basis for street-rod transporters.

PAGE 189: Fat-fendered rods out on the street in Reno, Nevada.

1974–76 Torino: the film required 12 cars, and the builders had to scour swap meets for the right type of alloy wheels. At the same time, the magazine was running a 1932 Deuce Roadster build-up series. *The Dukes of Hazzard* movie premiered in August 2005 and *Hot Rod* magazine featured an in-depth feature on the famous General Lee Dodge Charger, of which a total of 26 were used in making the film.

The 39th annual LA Roadsters Show in 2004 attracted no less than 800 entrants, while the 2005 NSRA Nationals were held in Louisville that year. The November 2005 issue of *Hot Rod* magazine didn't feature a single pre-1948 car, but it did cover some vintage drag-racing, and thoroughly detailed the flathead Ford V8. It also carried advertisements for the US Army at a time when it was committed to new operations in Iraq. In contrast, the December issue of *Hot Rod and Custom* magazine ran features on little else but pre-1948 cars, many of which were decidedly nostalgic in style. The

RIGHT & OPPOSITE: The curvaceous 1941 Willys coupé was frequently the basis of dragstrip gassers during the 1960s. This is a street-driven one, but it still features a blown V8 engine.

magazine also reported on the Thacker and Shine 1932 roadster's appearance at the noted Goodwood Festival of Speed in England. This, together with the appearance of hot rods at Pebble Beach, illustrates the level of acceptance by the classic car fraternity that the hot rod has managed to achieve. It only took 50 years!

The 1932 Ford, the car that brought style and performance to the mass market and went on to become the quintessential hot rod – the Deuce – will celebrate its 75th anniversary in 2007. Ford will be celebrating the 1932's impact on automotive history and culture with a display of 75 of the most influential and important, and will be selected by a panel of experts. The display will be unveiled at the January 2007 Grand National Roadster Show in Pomona, California, America's oldest annual hot-rod show. According to Larry Erickson, the Ford Motor Company's chief designer, 'The 1932 Ford continues to have a tremendous impact on many aspects of the automotive world and on contemporary culture. It was a landmark car for Ford Motor Company, beginning a period of styling dominance and, most significantly, offering the world's first mass-produced V8 engine. Then, years after its introduction, the 1932 Ford played a major role in another revolution – the development of the hot rod. These cast-off

cars, built in backyards and small garages, performed far beyond their original capabilities and often rivalled the performance of the best in the world. Hot rods are a uniquely American form of automotive expression.'

The 75 most influential will be selected by an experienced committee from a variety of fields. Museum participants include: Greg Sharp, curator; Wally Parks NHRA Motorsports Museum; Philip Linhares, chief curator of art, Oakland Museum of California; and Dick Messer, director of the Petersen Automotive Museum. Authors and journalists on the committee include Steve Coonan, publisher; *The Rodder's Journal*; John Dianna, publisher, *American Rodder*; Kevin Elliott, former editor of the British publication, *Custom Car*; Pat Ganahl, journalist and author of *Hot Rods & Cool Customs*, *Von Dutch: the Man*, *Myth & Legend*, and *Ford Performance*; Robert Genat, author, *Hot Rod Milestones*, *Little Deuce Coupé* and *The Birth of Hot Rodding*;

ABOVE: Not all street rods are Fords, as this 1935 Chevrolet shows.

OPPOSITE: This 1938 Ford pickup has pro-street styling, with huge rear-wheels and tyres contained within rear wheel-arches.

ABOVE LEFT: The 1957 Chevrolet pickup is a sought-after classic truck.

ABOVE: Woody styling looks good on fat-fendered rods.

LEFT: The Plymouth Prowler, a factory hot rod.

OPPOSITE: Typical 1990s treatment given to a 1932 three-window coupé.

Ken Gross, journalist, author of *Hot Rod Milestones*, and chief judge of the Pebble Beach Concours d'Élegance hot-rod class; Mark Morton, publisher, *Hop Up*; Tony Thacker, author, *'32 – The Deuce*; and Tom Vogele, vice president and group publisher, *Primedia*. Car-builders, designers and enthusiasts participating include musician and hot-rod collector Jeff Beck; Roy Brizio, Brizio Street Rods; Pete Chapouris, So-Cal Speed Shop; legendary hot-rodders Ray Brown, Pete Eastwood, Blackie Gejeian, Jim 'Jake' Jacobs and Thom Taylor; Jerry Kugel, Kugel Komponents; show promoter Robert Larivee, Sr; Barry Lobeck, V8 Shop; Gary Meadors, Goodguys Rod & Custom Association, and builder/historian David Simard. Erickson continues:'The list of '32

OPPOSITE: A Ford 1932 closed-cab pickup.

ABOVE LEFT: A 1932 Ford three-window coupé.

ABOVE: A Ford F-100 pickup.

LEFT: Interesting decoration on a pro-street Model A.

PAGE 198: A radical Ford coupé from 1934.

PAGE 199: A 1990s-style 1934 Ford two-door sedan.

Ford hot rods produced by this committee will be definitive. We'll reveal the panel's selections at the January 2006 Grand National Roadster Show, in lead-up to the display of actual cars at the 2007 anniversary show. Having these landmark vehicles together in one place for the first time will be an historic event.'

A number of other events, along with books written to honour the 1932 Ford, are planned and in production. Ford's list and display of the '75 Most Influential '32 Ford Hot Rods' is being designed to support and integrate with these other efforts. Ford will utilize the anniversary of its iconic model to celebrate the company's leadership in performance and styling, while tentative plans are being made for versions of the display to be shown at multiple venues. These include the Wally Parks NHRA Museum, the Petersen Automotive Museum, Pebble Beach Concours d'Élegance, the Specialty Equipment Manufacturers Association (SEMA) show and the Los Angeles International Auto Show.

RIGHT: The Duvall windshield is a timeless hot-rod component.

OPPOSITE: A subtly-chopped Model A coupé.

PAGE 202: A modified 1953 Chevrolet pickup.

PAGE 203: A pro-street Ford F-100 pickup.

CHAPTER NINE

HOT-ROD PEOPLE

ALEX XYDIAS

Pictured here at the So-Cal Speed Shop in 2005, Alex Xydias can look back over nearly 70 years of involvement in the hot-rod scene. He is undeniably a key figure in the movement that was born in Southern California, but which quickly spread to all parts of the world. An indication of the man's character is that he doesn't spend his time reminiscing about the 'good ol' days', but looks towards the future in his capacity as consultant to the new So-Cal, the company he originally founded in 1946.

Alex had been closely involved in hot-rodding well before the Second World War. He had driven a Model A roadster, while he was at high school, and had later acquired a pair of 1934 Fords, one a three-window coupé, the other a customized roadster. A member of the Sidewinders car club of Glendale, California, he had discovered the sport of dry-lakes racing well before the Japanese attack on Pearl Harbor propelled America into the war, causing young men in their teens and 20s to park up their cars and enlist in the military.

Alex joined the US Army Air Corps, working as an engineer on B-17 aircraft, and like many other hot-rodders, acquired skills that would serve him well after the

LEFT: The legendary Alex Xydias stands next to a belly-tank racer at the So-Cal workshop.

OPPOSITE ABOVE LEFT: Sixty five years separate the belly-tank racer from the 1934 Haas Roadster.

OPPOSITE ABOVE RIGHT: The Piersen Brothers' coupé is pushed to the start line.

OPPOSITE BELOW: The So-Cal belly tank is push-started at the beginning of a dry-lake record attempt.

war. It was during his military service that he decided what his life would be after he was demobbed: he would open a shop – not any old car shop, but a speed shop.

Speed shops existed prior to the Second World War, being establishments dedicated to enhancing car performance. They also sold bolt-on items, such as cylinder heads, manifolds, carburettors, cams, ignition systems, wheels and tyres, and were places where aficionados could hang out, kick tyres and swap tall stories. There, young wannabe hot-rodders could rub shoulders with the genuine article, men who raced their cars on dry lakes at Muroc and El Mirage. These racers told their tales of derring-do, while dicussing ways of making cars go faster.

In 1946 Alex was demobbed and

immediately set about establishing his own speed shop, which, while not the first in existence, would soon become the best-known, not only due to Alex's great promotional skills, but also as a result of his success as a dry-lakes record-breaker. Alex's shop was on Olive Avenue, in the Burbank district of Los Angeles, the name So-Cal being a common abbreviation of Southern California. Every day, Alex would park his 1934 Ford cabriolet outside the shop, as a way of drawing attention to his new venture, while inside, shelves were stacked high with bolt-on parts, such as chromed nuts, gauges, steel wheels and items usually supplied to the military, such as helmets and goggles. One day, Alex's 1934 cabriolet caught the eye of Dean Batchelor, who himself drove a 1932 roadster. Dean also raced his hot rod on the dry lakes, and was always on the look-out for promotional opportunities; Alex subsequently placed the So-Cal decal on the hood of Dean's 1932, and his first sponsorship deal was made.

Midget and roadster racing on oval tracks was popular at the time, attracting youngsters already interested in cars and speed. At the races, Alex not only stuck flyers advertising So-Cal to the windshields of every car in the parking lot, he also saw that the So-Cal name occupied a prominent

LEFT: The So-Cal 1927 roadster in action at El Mirage dry lake.

BELOW LEFT: A youthful Alex Xydias stands proudly beside his 1932 roadster.

OPPOSITE LEFT: Alex and his race-driver, Keith Baldwin, fettle the Model T roadster.

OPPOSITE RIGHT, ABOVE & BELOW: So-Cal's three-window coupé in action in 1952.

position in the race programmes.

Being a hot-rodder himself, the next logical step was for him to build and race his own So-Cal car, figuring that speed records were a sure-fire way to draw attention to his business, and set it apart from the competition. Alex bought a Sears prefabricated double garage, which he erected on a lot on the aptly-named Victory Boulevard; this provided him with a place where he could build a race car, as well as sell his ever-increasing range of performance accessories. Ever conscious of the need to stand out from the crowd, he decided to build a belly-tank racer, which he would enter in the fastest streamliner class at the dry lakes.

Belly-tank cars had developed as a direct result of the war, belly tanks being external fuel tanks designed to extend the operational range of fighter aircraft, such as

the P-51 Mustang and P-38 Lightning. They were attached to the fuselage and wings of the aircraft and were discarded when empty, hence their alternative name, 'drop tank'. They were made of aluminium and were shaped like teardrops to minimize drag and maximize aerodynamics. Legend has it that their application to cars came about when a hot-rodder and racer from before the war, Bill Burke, joined the Coast Guard as his contribution to the war effort. One day, he saw a barge-full of belly tanks being towed out to sea, and was immediately struck by their potential future as streamliners.

As soon as he got out of the services in 1946, Bill sourced a belly tank in a scrapyard and built the very first belly-tank racer. There were two sizes of tank, 165- and 315-gallon. The latter, used on the P-38 Lightnings, was seen as more suitable, as it measured 36in (91cm) in diameter. This enabled the builder to install a flathead V8 into the rear half, leaving room for a driver

OPPOSITE: The So-Cal Model T roadster at El Mirage in 1950.

ABOVE: The So-Cal streamliner in action on Daytona Beach.

to squeeze into the front. These belly-tank racers were later piloted by the legendary Wally Parks.

Alex turned to Bill for the chassis of a race-car, based on a Model T Ford frame. A P-38 belly tank was purchased for $15 and a V-8 60 engine was chosen: it was small, but it could still utilize hopped-up parts from the larger flathead, with the result that the So-Cal belly-tank racer clocked up a run of 87mph (140km/h) on its shake-down run in 1948. By the end of that year, it had taken the record in the A Streamliner class to over 130mph (209km/h). The belly-tank racer pictured in So-Cal's workshop, on page 204, is actually the second one built by Alex Xydias, and restored to its present glory by Pete Chapouris, the first having been broken down and used to build a super-fast streamliner.

The Southern California Timing

LEFT: The infamous streamliner became known as the world's fastest hot rod.

BELOW: In 1952 the So-Cal team was named number one by Mechanix magazine and featured on the front cover.

OPPOSITE: The streamliner is push-started, prior to a record attempt on Daytona Beach.

Association (SCTA) had been obliged to relinquish its use of an airfield near Muroc to the USAF, so it was constantly on the lookout for new sites for speed tests, and the vast salt flats at Bonneville, near Wendover, Utah, were a possibility. They had been used for attempts on exotic land-speed records by people such as Sir Malcom Campbell, but when the SCTA approached the American Automobile Association (AAA), it was turned down, on the grounds that speeds achieved at Bonneville could never be matched by a mere hot rod. Early in 1949 Wally Parks decided to bypass the AAA and arranged a meeting with the Salt Lake City Chamber of Commerce which, impressed by the professionalism of the SCTA, granted it a time-trial event, the first of the Bonneville National Speed Trials.

Alex was excited at the prospect of racing at such an historic venue, and influenced by the wind-tunnel science of European Grand Prix cars, decided to build a special streamliner for Bonneville. Utilizing the chassis from the first belly-tank, Neil Emory, of Valley Custom, fabricated the aluminium bodywork. No one took them seriously, but Alex and his So-Cal racing team were about to enter the record books, creating hot-rod history. Until then, top speeds achieved by hot rods had been in the region of 150mph (240km/h), but the So-Cal streamliner, driven by Dean Batchelor, clocked 193mph (310km/h) in its record run, and in 1950 increased that time to 210mph (338km/h). Not only did it go on to better the record by 50mph in only two years, it was also the fastest American car ever built. For the next few years, So-Cal's was the most successful team in dry-lakes speed trials.

In 1952 the So-Cal team appeared on the cover of *Best Hot Rods*, the cars sporting the team colours of white with red scallops. The following year, the So-Cal coupé ran 172mph (277km/h) at Bonneville, running a blown flathead in the C Comp

coupé class. In 1954 *Hot Rod* magazine referred to the coupé as the 'double-threat coupé': this is because it had set records at both Bonneville and at the quarter-mile drag strip at Pomona, where it ran 121mph (195km/h) without a supercharger, achieving a Class B modified record. It was around this time that the overhead-valve engines were coming to the fore, making life difficult for the flathead boys.

Alex decided to change his focus, becoming increasingly involved in making films to document the hot-rod scene at Bonneville and the drags – also at the Pike's Peak hill climb and the NASCAR races. To a degree he had been influenced in this by his father, who was already involved in silent movies. Alex's long-term business partner, Keith Baldwin, dealt with the day-to-day running of the speed shop, while

Alex concentrated on making the business a success. When Keith left in 1961, the So-Cal Speed Shop was closed down, though it was never ever forgotten. Rather than being the end of an era, it merely signalled the end of another phase in Alex Xydias' life; he was destined to be involved in cars and racing for many more years to come.

In 1963 Alex met Dick Day, the publisher of *Car Craft* magazine, who

offered him a job which he accepted: Alex was the magazine's editor for a year before moving on to Petersen's publication, *Hot Rod Industry News.* While editor of this publication, he was instrumental in setting up the High Performance and Custom Equipment Trade Show in 1967. The show was held outdoors, under the grandstands of the Dodgers Stadium. As Alex remarked at the time, 'It was cold and dark, but it was a start'. The second show was held in the

Anaheim Convention Center, having been endorsed by the fledgling Specialty Equipment Market Association (SEMA). By now it was the official SEMA show and Alex was its director.

Over the next few years, the show grew too large for Anaheim, resulting in Alex and the SEMA board moving it to Las Vegas, where it is still held each year. Alex was included in the SEMA Hall of Fame in 1982, and retired in 1987, while retaining close ties

with the car world. He continues to attend all SEMA's shows to this day.

Alex's retirement heralded yet another phase in the life of a man committed to car performance. In 1997, with Pete Chapouris, he resurrected the legendary So-Cal Speed Shop, and the famous red-and-white So-Cal logo once again appeared over the door of a hot-rod workshop in Pomona, thus ensuring that the story would continue. So-Cal continues to chase Bonneville records and set

OPPOSITE: Note the hasty improvisations that have been made to this roadster, utilizing cardboard boxes and duct (duck) tape to gain a few more mph.

BELOW: The So-Cal line-up makes an impressive sight at El Mirage in 1951.

new standards of excellence under the directorship of Pete Chapouris and the consultancy of Alex Xydias.

PETE CHAPOURIS

Pete's father was a hot-rodder, so no one was surprised when his son followed in his tyre-tracks and began to cruise the boulevards of Los Angeles in 1955. At that time, Pete drove a 1932 roadster – not a car that was cherished or sought-after in those days – and he sold the body for $50, replacing it with that of a Model A coupé, and adding a Chevy V8 engine. Pete was then working in the field of electronic instruments, even though his real interest was in hot rods and dragsters. Lacking the necessary skills to pursue his dream, he went to night classes to learn welding, and eventually got a part-time job with M&S Welding, building dragsters.

In 1971 Pete took the plunge and went to work full-time for Blair's Speed Shop, a well-established outfit with a good reputation in the performance business. Pete chopped down a 1934 coupé, which he painted black, adorning the hood with the classic flame design, that licked along each side of the car. He was unaware at the time that the car would change his life: it appeared on the cover of the November 1973 issue of *Rod & Custom* magazine, together with another chopped 1934 coupé, painted vivid yellow, which had been built by Jim 'Jake' Jacobs. Pete and

RIGHT: Martin Sheen sits on the running-board of The California Kid hot rod, in a break from filming.

OPPOSITE: Pete Chapouris built the 1934 three-window coupé, California Kid, which achieved fame in the TV movie of the same name.

Jake were introduced to one another and immediately recognized how much they had in common, especially where hot rods were concerned. They soon figured out a way of working together, and with Eric Vaughan, established Auto Rejuvenation, in Temple City, which evolved into Pete & Jake's Hot Rod Repair shop.

Pete admits that times were hard, and that it was often a struggle to make ends meet. So much so, that when Pete got a phone call from TV producer, Howie Horowitz, asking if he could borrow Pete's 1934 coupé for a TV movie, he almost turned him down, feeling he could not afford to lose out on work by leaving the shop. Fortunately, Pete decided to drive the coupé over to Universal Studios after all, and the rest is history.

The movie starred the young Martin Sheen as the California Kid, this being the

LEFT: Alex Xydias and Pete Chapouris pictured at the current So-Cal workshop.

ABOVE: A Deuce roadster takes shape at So-Cal.

OPPOSITE ABOVE LEFT: The Haas team's Bonneville roadster is actually street-legal.

OPPOSITE ABOVE RIGHT: The much-modified Chevy HHR Suburban is powered by a GM Ecotec turbocharged 2.0-litre motor, producing 800hp.

OPPOSITE BELOW LEFT: This Chevrolet Cobalt is also part of So-Cal and GM's race team. It ran 243mph (391km/h) at Bonneville in 2004.

OPPOSITE BELOW RIGHT: The So-Cal special 1932 roadster is actually all-new, featuring a Brookville roadster body in a step-boxed chassis.

ABOVE and RIGHT: The So-Cal Ecotec lakester is a modern-day tribute to the belly-tank lakester raced by Alex Xydias in the early 1950s. It is powered by an almost stock supercharged 2.0-litre Ecotec engine, setting a record of 179.3mph (288.5km/h) in the blown gas lakester class at Bonneville.

OPPOSITE: A So-Cal special Deuce roadster, built entirely from new parts and ready for delivery.

legend on the car he drove into town to avenge his father's death at the hands of the local sheriff, played by Vic Morrow. The movie, with its dramatic car chase along canyon roads north of Los Angeles, was to introduce the hot rod to mainstream America. Pete's 1934 coupé was the real star of the show, however, and has been known as the California Kid ever since.

This exposure gave a welcome boost to Pete and Jake's business, which rapidly gained a reputation as one of the best. They continued to build exceptional cars that featured in hundreds of hot-rod magazines until 1987, when Pete & Jake's Hot Rod Repair shop was sold.

After this, Pete went to work for SEMA as director of marketing. He continued there

for three years, but the lure of the workshop was proving too strong, and he teamed up with Bob Bauder to form Syntassien in 1990. Around this time, Pete met the guitarist Billy Gibbons, of the Texas rock band ZZ Top, building for him a pair of Harley-Davidson 'HogZZillas', the first of many such assignments for Gibbons, which continue to this day. In 1995 Pete opened up PC3g (the Pete Chapouris group) on Grand Avenue, Pomona. This was destined to become one of the best hot-rod shops in the world, building not only cutting-edge hot rods from the ground up, but also restoring important historic hot rods and racers.

Bruce Meyer is the world's foremost collector of historic hot rods, and a part of his collection can be seen at the Petersen Museum in Los Angeles. The first car PC3g restored for him was the Pierson brothers' coupé, arguably the best-known hot-rod race car of them all. Another key restoration was Doane Spencer's 1932 Ford roadster, which in the late 1940s was in a class of its own, having a standard of finish that was second to none. It was glossy black, with a Duvall windshield, solid hood, hairpin front radius rods and 1937 Ford teardrop tail lights. Spencer raced it on both the dry lakes and the street and even made several cross-country journeys. In 1950 he prepared the car for the Carrera Panamericana road race in Mexico; Doane fitted 16-in (41-cm) wheels and Lincoln drum brakes, and in order to achieve greater ground clearance, raised the engine and gas tank and ran the exhaust pipes through the frame rails. He achieved the classic 'highboy' look, that future Deuce builders would continue to

emulate to the present day. After the restoration was complete, the roadster won the inaugural hot-rod class at the revered Pebble Beach Concours d'Élegance in 1997, the first time 'outlaw' hot-rodders had been allowed onto the hallowed lawns.

When Bruce Meyer acquired the second

So-Cal belly-tank racer, then in a sorry state, he naturally turned to Pete's shop to carry out its restoration. In the course of the restoration, Bruce Meyer introduced Alex Xydias to Pete, a meeting that would spark another chapter in hot-rodding history, and revive the legendary So-Cal name. Although it had been over 30

years since Alex Xydias closed the So-Cal Speed Shop down, he had always retained ownership of the name.

Pete had long felt that PC3g (his initials, with 3g referring to three generations of Petes in his family) did not quite work in a marketing sense, and was looking for

OPPOSITE: The Pierson brothers' coupé undergoes restoration by the team at So-Cal.

LEFT: The coupé was taken to the UK and paraded before fans at the Goodwood Festival of Speed.

BELOW LEFT: The Pierson coupé is part of Bruce Meyer's hot-rod collection, and can be seen at the Petersen Museum.

BELOW: This is the old So-Cal coupé, as raced by Jim Travis in the 1990s.

something to replace it. Alex had recently reprinted his So-Cal catalogues from the 1940s, and was selling them as nostalgic mementoes. Pete jokingly suggested that Alex resurrect So-Cal at PC3g, and to his astonishment Alex said, when do we start? That was back in 1997, when the famous red-and-white So-Cal logo went up over the door of 1357E Grand Avenue, Pomona.

Pete could visualize how he and his crew would restore famous old hot rods, build show-winning cars and, best of all, go racing again on the dry lakes of Southern California under the So-Cal banner. His vision went beyond the world of traditional rodding: his ambition was to bring the story right up to date and build high-technology modern cars relevant to the 21st century.

A look around the So-Cal workshops in 2005 confirms the realization of Pete's vision: in one workshop, an unlikely vehicle – a Chevy HHR (Heritage High Roof) sits, GM's tribute to the 1949 Chevy Suburban: needless to say, it didn't stay a 'High Roof' for long. In another corner stands a modern car, a Chevrolet Cobalt SS coupé, and in another a modern version of Alex Xydias' belly-tank racer, while elsewhere in the workshop is a 1934 roadster that has been given the high-tech treatment. All four have something in common: they all sport the classic So-Cal red-and-white livery, but what is more significant is that they are all powered by different versions of GM's Ecotec engine.

Pete Chapouris and So-Cal have been able to achieve something that a few years ago would have seemed impossible – a hot-rod speed shop teamed with one of the largest auto manufacturers in the world. This certainly emphasizes the regard and respect that have been earned by Pete's team at So-Cal, and the professionalism and experience they are now able to bring to the table. How different from the early days, when hot-rodders were seen as outlaws and outsiders, cutting up and chopping down street vehicles in an effort to gain extra speed.

So how did this seemingly unlikely association come about? According to Mark Reuss, the executive director of GM's Performance Division, it was almost by chance: he had seen So-Cal cars on the cover of a magazine and wanted to make the pedal car he had bought for his three-year-old son resemble a 1932 roadster. Mark approached

So-Cal for paint and stickers, and later sent a video of the finished article to the company. Reuss met up with Pete Chapouris at the 2002 SEMA show in Las Vegas and, in the course of conversation, Pete mentioned how he would like to re-invent the lakester as a tribute to Alex Xydias, So-Cal's founder, and begin dry-lakes racing once again. This interested Mark, who saw an opportunity to involve GM in grass-roots competition and associate itself with the strong American tradition of racing at Bonneville. GM also wanted to utilize its stock four-cylinder Ecotec engine, in 2.0-, 2.2- and 2.4-litre capacities, that ranged in power from 140 to 1000bhp when supercharged. In 2005 GM and So-Cal took four cars to the races, all Ecotec-powered, and all sporting the red-and-white So-Cal livery, first used over 60 years ago.

The HHR cabriolet had represented GM's entry into the small front-wheel-drive SUV market. Before it could be raced on the salt, however, much modification was required, which was performed by the So-Cal crew. The roof was chopped by 7in (18cm) and the body was lengthened by 4in (10cm), while the chassis was replaced by a chrome-molybdenum tubular double rail, more commonly found on Pro-Mod dragsters. The engine was resited in a central position, in the place where the front seats would have been, in line with the longitudinal axis of the car. The driver sat in the back and the fuel tank was in the front, achieving better weight distribution as a result. The nose of the HHR was restyled and fabricated in fibreglass by So-Cal, thus improving streamlining.

In 2005 the HHR was campaigned at Bonneville by the manager of GM's Engineering Group, Jim Minneker, in the G/Blown Fuel Altered coupé class. At the August 2005 Bonneville Speedweek, the HHR ran 208.690mph (335.845km/h) on a rough surface, but an attempt at 226.835mph could not be made due to poor weather conditions.

The other cars, campaigned by GM-So-Cal, consisted of a Chevrolet Cobalt SS, an Ecotec Lakester, and the 1934 Haas Racing Roadster, all running 2.0-litre Ecotec engines, the SS and roadster being turbocharged and intercooled, producing 800bhp, while the lakester was supercharged and delivered about 300bhp.

The Ecotec Lakester pays homage to the famous belly-tank racer built by Alex Xydias, which ran up to 198mph (319km/h) in the early 1950s. The body is not made from an aluminium drop tank, but is of modern composite materials, surrounded by a Top Fuel-style chassis. The aeronautical connection is still there, however, represented by the F-16 fighter-style cockpit canopy, reinforced by the airplane-style tailpiece.

The Haas Racing Roadster harks directly back to the style of the old hot rods. The Ecotec engine is not only supplied by GM, it also comes with GM's technical support. The car set a new G/Blown Fuel Roadster record of 193mph (311km/h) in 2004, and most surprisingly can be driven on the street, a fact demonstrated by the Haas team, when it drove the car 700 miles (1126km) from Pomona to Bonneville, before laying the blue

OPPOSITE LEFT: Jimmy 'Shine' Falschlehner heads the 'outlaw' division at So-Cal.

OPPOSITE RIGHT: Jimmy Shine's 1934 Ford pickup, Bare Nekkid, is one of the most recognized rat rods in the USA.

tarpaulin on the salt, making a few race-trim adjustments, and going racing, for all the world like the hard-core hot-rodders of the 1940s and '50s.

Meanwhile, in the 21st century, the So-Cal Speed Shop is still doing justice to its rich heritage, while continuing to push back the technological boundaries and make cars go even faster.

JIMMY 'SHINE' FALSCHLEHNER
Jimmy Shine is a surfer/punk-rocker, a builder of custom Harley-Davidsons and a hot-rodder. Now working for So-Cal's 'outlaw' division, Jimmy is fast becoming a media star, thanks to the popularity of TV reality shows featuring hot-rod builders. He recently came to prominence on Discovery channel's Hot-Rod Build-Off series, in which Jimmy, the young upstart, was pitted against Barry White, an established top-class builder. Jimmy stole the show in one memorable sequence that showed him surfing along the side of a flooded highway, towed by a pickup truck, after a sudden rainstorm had hit the area. This indicates Jimmy Shine's abundant 'urban cool'.

Pete Chapouris recognized Jimmy's potential and talent early on, realizing that

the only thing needed was to rein-in the young tattooed rebel, and allow him to do what he did best, build cool old-school hot rods, which would appeal to the ever-increasing band of young rat-rodders. So-Cal now features Jimmy Shine merchandise in its catalogue, and there is no shortage of buyers. At a recent hot-rod run in London, England, Jimmy Shine t-shirts and baseball hats were very much in evidence, emphasizing the renewed international interest in hot rods, and especially the old-school cool, which Jimmy personifies.

The 1934 Ford pickup, pictured here, is undoubtedly Jimmy's signature vehicle. Finished in bare metal and slammed to the ground, the truck exudes style and attitude. Some would refer to it as a rat rod, an example of the popular unfinished or primer cars favoured by rockabilly hot-rodders, but

it is a mistake to think of them as badly built or poorly finished, especially in the case of Jimmy Shine's truck, which he calls 'Bare Nekkid'. This truck is well crafted and engineered and displays Jimmy's knack for using interesting combinations of components. This is what he had to say:

'Bare Nekkid, the '34 Ford pickup, was another piece of crap car I picked up for $500. '34 chassis, '34 cab. It had a '32 bed on it, which I passed on to the Kennedy brothers. It was a beat piece of crap! It had no floor, no firewall, no dash, the doors were just junk! I brought this thing to the shop on a trailer and Pete said – why don't you just take that thing straight to the dump? – I said, no, I can fix this thing. I have sketches and drawings from about 10–15 years ago that I did at school. I had the idea back then to build that car. I chopped it 5 inches,

OPPOSITE: Jimmy Shine's Bare Nekkid is not thrown together, but actually consists of many hand-made items that have been expertly engineered.

BELOW: The shiniest part of the truck is the V8 flathead motor, which boasts polished slash-cut air stacks, cooling pipes and zoomie exhaust headers.

RIGHT: Jimmy Shine also builds classy Harley-Davidson custom bikes. In 2005 he presented his latest, a Springer Panhead, to the public in Sturgis.

channeled it 6 inches. I set the cab a little further back on the chassis. I didn't use a Ford bed, the lines are wrong. I wanted to do a stubby bed, but the lines where the fenders go around the wheels were wrong. So I made my own bed, designed all my own belt lines into it. I didn't like the square edges on the bed rails of the '30 trucks. I didn't like the square stake pockets, so I used '40 Ford stake pockets and riveted them on. I used '53 Studebaker header panels to go on the front of the bed, they've got this really bitchin' roll, so I used those for the sides as well as the header panel. I cut and raked the rails of the frame at the back to get the car to ride real low. In the front I used a Model A cross member and So-Cal hairpins, but I made my

spring and shackles attach to the hairpins and my axle sat out in front.

'My car is kind of unique in that way, that my axle's out in front, it's totally clean, no springs, no anything, it also makes it sit really low. I mounted the motor and transmission really high in the car, so if you look at my car from down low, there's nothing visible below the chassis, nothing will drag the ground underneath my car. I had to make all my own steering rods, which I put together piece-by-piece. The wheels are a combination. I would really have liked to have run 18-inch milk-truck wheels, like on the back of the old belly-tank racer, but they're really super rare, and

if you can find them, they are very expensive. But I wanted to run 18-inch wheels all around it, something kind of artillery, spokey, funky. I came across those rim centers at G&J Aircraft, lying in the back lot. I measured the drop center, it was $16\frac{1}{2}$ inches, and that's the drop center for an 18-inch wheel. I measured the bolt pattern, and it was the same as an early Ford. I didn't know what they were of, but Cliff of G&J gave them to me. It turns out they were off a '32 Studebaker President. I brought them back to the shop here and cut the hoops off them, and a guy at Circle One Racing Wheels spun up some hoops for me, with rim-widths of $4\frac{1}{2}$ inches in the front

and $5\frac{1}{4}$ in the rear. The spoke centers I found fitted right inside those rims, so I jig-welded them in, and I had this spoke wheel and a new hoop that were perfectly flat. I cut a Ford wire wheel, cut all the spokes off, drilled it and riveted it in so I could have Ford hub caps.

'The fuel tank is sited in the pickup bed and is made out of a B-52 bomber hydraulic tank. It took a while to locate a usable flathead V8. It's a 1949 8BA with Edelbrock heads and an intake supporting twin '97s, and I hand-made the carb stacks. The headers are also hand-made chromed zoomies. The steering column is hand-crafted, as is the pedal assembly. The dash

ABOVE LEFT: A customer's classic Ford is treated to a new motor and transmission, courtesy of Jimmy Shine.

ABOVE: A 1935 Ford truck belonging to Billy Gibbons of the ZZ Top rock band.

OPPOSITE: This Hiboy 1932 roadster is a joint venture of the Kennedy brothers and Jimmy Shine.

is out of a 1940 Ford and the seats are aircraft ejector buckets.

'All in all, it turned out to be a pretty cool truck – people seem to like it. One guy even built an exact replica of it, although I

don't know why anyone with talent would just copy my truck instead of doing something original.

'Billy Gibbons of ZZ Top is a good friend and a customer of ours, and he really digs my truck. He tried to buy it off me, but it's not for sale. We're going to build him another truck in a similar style soon.'

There is little doubt that Jimmy Shine has built a landmark hot rod, which will be remembered alongside other famous cars, such as the Pierson brothers' coupé, Ed Roth's Outlaw, the California Kid, and ZZ Top's Cadzilla.

Jimmy now describes how it all started: 'I had a crazy passion for cars as a kid,

blame it on my Dad, who used to be into hot rods and motorcycles before he moved on into sand rails and boats. I didn't care about sports, soccer/baseball, still don't, I was only interested in cars. I made a go-cart when I was six or seven, my Dad helped me weld it. I had to save my money to get it done. At 13 years old I bought a '40 Willys pickup truck, 950 bucks – I had saved my money up for years. My attitude was, I am going to build a hot rod!

'We had an oxyacetylene tank in the garage, an arc welder and drill press, very basic tools. By this time my Dad was into boats, but they made me seasick. Besides, I only cared about cars and reading *Hot Rod*

magazine. I had a motorcycle and got chased by the cops. I had a few friends, but not many, I was an automotive oddball. The instructor in "shop" class was an idiot, he didn't know anything. He tried to show me how to do something – I thought, you gotta be kidding me – watch this! I got a really bad grade in metal shop. When I was 16, I had built my own '40 Willys pickup truck. Small black Chevy, turbo 400, narrowed 9 inches, designed my own four-link suspension, built a tube chassis for it. I even painted it in my parents' garage. So when I was 16, I was driving like a pro-street car, pretty crazy.

'I had two jobs, I went to a sheetmetal shop after school, and I worked in an engine shop across the street as well. I would work one hour from like 3–4, then they closed, and then I'd go across the street and work at this engine shop rebuilding motors and heads. That's when I built my own motors. I'd be there from about 4–6pm, then they would close, and I would hang out there afterwards and work on my own stuff. I built all my own sheetmetal work at the first shop, built tailgates, firewalls, body panels, floors. I had a key when I was 14 years old to get into that sheetmetal shop anytime I wanted. It was union-owned and I had a key to the place at 14. I used to sweep the floors, and had a key to the place; the boss thought I was cool – come in here anytime you like, do anything you want! Vince at Pacific Auto Parts, the engine shop, always let me go there and do whatever I wanted. He'd help me build my own stuff, and teach me to use the various machines and tools,

LEFT: This roadster belongs to Billy Gibbons of ZZ Top, and is only one of a collection of hot rods owned by the Texan rock star.

and I also swept the floor and delivered parts, it was a great experience.

'So then I sold the Willy's truck and started building a chopped '48 Anglia, the first car I ever chopped – I think I screwed it up pretty bad. I ditched finals in junior high school because I was too busy chopping my car. I built a chopped Model A when I was in high school. I had a '55 Chevy truck with a big block and a four-speed, which I then traded in for a '47 Indian Chief basket case, which I built up. It turned out to be stolen, and I got arrested and went to jail for that. My Mom had to bail me out – it was bullshit, man.

'I worked for a Harley shop in Glendale, I worked on a bike for Bruce Springsteen – another for Billy Idol. I had an Ossa dirt bike, my ole Indian, and then I built a rigid Panhead when I was 18. Then I dropped out altogether at 21, went to Mexico, went surfing. I had a custom '52 Chevy pickup truck that was slammed, which I drove every day. I dropped out of the scene for about five years, I guess, didn't do a whole lot of anything much. This was after my first wife divorced me. I re-emerged about '96 and hung around a few bike shops, and I heard that Pete Chapouris was looking to hire someone. I thought there wasn't much chance that he'd hire me. I was real intimidated coming here to So-Cal.'

THACKER & SHINE'S ROADSTER

In keeping with the spirit of the original So-Cal Speed Shop, Tony Thacker and Jimmy Shine have been developing a street roadster, which they could also race on the dry lakes.

The car, a 1928 Model A Ford roadster body on an original 1932 chassis, was originally built by New Zealander Steve Davies, of the So-Cal race shop in the late 1990s. He also drove it on the road to and from races, and at dry lakes such as El Mirage and Muroc, where he set records, taking a D-class street roadster at 165mph (266km/h) in 1997. Since taking over the matt-black roadster, Thacker and Shine drove the 800 miles (1290km) to Bonneville in 2002, ran 180mph (290km/h), then drove 800 miles home again.

Tony Thacker, responsible for PR and marketing at So-Cal, sees it as a tribute to the hot-rodders of 1946, who regularly drove their street rods to the lakes, raced them, and with luck, successfully drove home again.

After achieving 181mph, the goal posts were moved and the aim of the Thacker and Shine team was to run 200mph, thus joining a very exclusive club. However, a new motor was needed before they could achieve their goal. For this, Pete Chapouris, boss of So-Cal, removed the motor from his personal roadster: the small-block blown Chevy was then sent to the legendary engine-tuner, John

Tony Thacker and Jimmy Shine's 1928 roadster has been built into a 1932 chassis and was taken to 201mph (323.5km/h) by Jimmy at Bonneville.

Beck, of Pro Machine in California, who rebuilt the engine and fitted Pro Action cast-iron heads, the engine delivering a respectable 741 horses on the dyno after this treatment. In 2003, Thacker and Shine drove the roadster to Bonneville, a journey so comfortable that Tony claims to have fallen asleep while Jimmy was driving.

Arriving at the salt flats, near Wendover, Utah, they met up with their race crew, who proceeded to prep the car for the following day's racing. This involved changing the road tyres to 18-in (46-cm) Dunlop road-

ABOVE: Thacker and Shine drove the roadster from So-Cal in Los Angeles to Bonneville in Utah, a distance of over 700 miles. Here the mechanics are making a few alterations to the car in preparation for a speed-record attempt.

RIGHT: Echoes of 1946, the Thacker and Shine roadster on the vast salt flats of Bonneville.

OPPOSITE: Tony Thacker took the roadster to the Goodwood Festival of Speed in the UK, where it was driven around the circuit to the delight of classic race-car fans.

racing tyres on the rear and 16-in Goodyear Bonneville racing tyres on the front. The windshield was removed and a fibreglass tonneau cover fitted to cover the passenger area and facilitate streamlining. The road suspension was replaced with rigid struts, and the exhaust changed to open zoomies. A Mert Littlefield 8-71 blower was fitted along with hi-flow fuel lines and pump to supply the go-juice in sufficient quantities for a high-speed run.

On the first run, the gearbox let go at 182mph (293km/h) and had to be rebuilt overnight. Then Jimmy Shine drove the roadster to 192mph (309km/h), the only problem being that he went through the timing lights backwards, as a result of a spin. Driving a car in a straight line at nearly 200mph is not as straightforward as some would think; the salt layer varies in smoothness from event to event, and often has to be graded by the race organizers before the next race can take place. If a car is running low in the race order, it will encounter ruts and soft spots created by earlier cars. All this, of course, affects the car's stability and its potential top speed: it takes a brave man to go out again after spinning out at 192mph, but Jimmy Shine has certainly got what it takes.

In August 2004 Thacker and Shine realized their dream, when Jimmy drove the roadster to 201mph (323.5km/h) at the Bonneville National Speed Week, a feat achieved possibly by only three other street-legal hot rods. It is good to know that the pioneering spirit of the old hot-rodders is still going strong, thanks to So-Cal and enthusiasts such as Tony Thacker and Jimmy Shine.

THE KENNEDY BROTHERS

The 1932 Deuce coupés and roadsters are regarded as the ultimate cars to chop by serious hot-rod aficionados. The unique body style looked great when fenders were removed and they were smaller and lighter than in subsequent years, and therefore potentially faster. Finding vintage tin gets harder year on year, though even seemingly hopeless rust boxes can be restored and rodded, there being nothing cooler than the real thing, even if most of the original metal has to be replaced. Only 12–14,000 roadsters were manufactured by Ford in 1932.

In Los Angeles, no conversation about 1932 Fords and parts goes on for long before a name crops up, that of the Kennedy brothers. Joe and Jason Kennedy gained much of their mechanical know-how from their father, a classic car restorer, and it is from his workshop, which they inherited, that they ply their trade, building and repairing 1932 Ford hot rods: nothing else will do and only 1932 models ever get a look-in.

RIGHT: The Kennedy brothers, Jason and Joe, pictured in their yard, surrounded by their stockpile of panels and parts, which they use in their hot-rod projects.

OPPOSITE LEFT: Jason's personal project, a 1932 five-window coupé.

OPPOSITE RIGHT: 'Chopper' Lance is well-known in hot-rod circles, since he appeared on the TV RIDES show on Discovery Channel.

They have been in business for 12 years now, although when meeting them, they do not seem old enough to have been around that long. They are quiet, polite, softly-spoken guys, who would not look out of place among the surfing fraternity. Don't expect to find them advertised in any hot-rod magazine; their reputation is such that they do not need to publicize themselves – reputation and word-of-mouth gets them all the work they need. In fact, finding their workshop can be problematical, as they do not even have a sign up over their door, but if you are driving high enough, say in a SUV, you might be able to spot the rusty old donor cars parked in their yard, giving a clue to

their whereabouts. The Kennedy premises are modest, being a collection of single-storey buildings combining workshops and storage space with a reception/chill-out area, which houses the brothers' collection of 'cool stuff' – old surf boards, skateboards, classic bicycles, old rail drag racers and general auto memorabilia.

The brothers are ably assisted by well-known hot-rodder, 'Chopper' Lance, from Burbank, who famously appeared on a RIDES TV programme featuring a hot-rod build. All-in-all, the atmosphere at the Kennedys' shop is laid-back and calm, there being no sign of pressure – evident at many other shops. This is what Jason had to say:

'We build '32 Fords, that's it, no '34s, no '36s. If anyone asks we say, sorry we're fully occupied with '32 jobs. We prefer to build '32 hot rods the way they were put together in the '50s era. All the parts you see here, all the parts that we buy in are all '32 parts. We like the '32, it's the most popular with the traditional hot-rodders. It's a neat, simple car, easy to work on. Wherever possible, we like to work with original bodies and chassis, but we will use repop bodies like the Brookville roadster and sometimes the customer may want to use a newly-manufactured chassis, like the one made by So-Cal Speed Shop. In fact, we just finished a joint '32 roadster project with Jimmy Shine of So-Cal, using

one of their chassis. Jimmy prepared the chassis and engine over at So-Cal and brought it over here, where we fitted the Brookville body and painted it as well. We fitted an original '32 steering column, a shifter, original dash and Duvall windshield. We wired it up and got it going. We did not fit the interior upholstery, So-Cal arranged for that to be done. We went to a lot of trouble to make the roadster look original, even down to drilling in holes where the fenders and running boards would have been fitted on an original chassis. That's the kind of attention to detail that we put into a project, in fact most average guys out there wouldn't be able to tell whether the finished

car is original or repro. We don't mind using the Brookville roadster body if a customer hasn't got an original, it's the best out there and it's metal. We won't work on any fiberglass bodies, we just don't want to know about those plastic things! However, we prefer to work with original '32 bodies and chassis and fit all original parts – we find that the original stuff just works better, it goes together right – while the repop stuff doesn't always go together right, without a bit of reworking.

'It's getting harder to come by original tin, but everything is available in California, it's just a question of price. If you need it right away, you're going to pay a premium, but if you've got time and patience, something will come up at a good price – you just need that patience. We don't go looking for parts at swap meets; as you can see, we've got our own swap meet right here in the yard! We have our own small network, so if a customer comes in looking for a '32 five-window, we can call people we know. If they don't have it, they soon find out about someone who has, and we soon get to know about it.

'As for the motors, we prefer to work with the flathead V8s of the period. We don't do any major mechanical work on the motors, but we do fit heads, manifolds, intakes and carbs. We can paint cars here, but we do send some cars out to be painted. We don't do upholstery.

LEFT: Lance helps solve a carburation problem on the coupé.

ABOVE: A 1932 three-window coupé takes shape in the Kennedy brothers' workshop in Pomona, California.

OPPOSITE: Jason Kennedy preferred not to chop the roof of his car, a common modification to many a hot-rod coupé.

'We like the fact that customers see what we do and ask us to do the same for them. That's how we prefer to work, people asking us to do things the way we like to do them, that is the right way for the period of the car. We always aim to stay true to the period in which the car was built. So if it's a '50s-style roadster we will only use parts and accessories that would have been available then, no mix and match stuff from different periods. We prefer to use V8 flatheads, but we will fit early overhead-valve engines of the correct period if the customer wants it. If a customer comes in and wants fuel injection or something, we say no, you'll have to go somewhere else for that.

'Our customers know how we work and what we're prepared to do. We don't get involved with the type of customer who wants to come in and call the shots and change this and that, and then bring in his buddies to create a kind of committee car. We don't get involved with car shows or magazines. We don't mind if they come around, but we prefer to stay as low-key as possible – we don't go looking for publicity.

'We get a lot of attention from the Swedish magazines for some reason. I think So-Cal sends them over here because the Swedish are very interested in the early original-style stuff that we're into, while So-Cal is into a lot of modern stuff these days.

'Yeah, we're really happy with what we're doing, concentrating on '32 hot rods, doing them right like they were back in the day and being kind of laid-back about it.'

TROY LADD of HOLLYWOOD HOT RODS

Many hot-rodders of the 1960s and '70s are still running shops today in 2005, proving that once a hot-rodder, always a hot-rodder. It's a close-knit community, and everyone knows everyone else and the kind of work they turn out. Consequently, as a newcomer,

it is difficult to penetrate their ranks. A good reputation is fiercely won in this demanding group; hot-rodders have high standards and codes of behaviour that it would be wise to understand if one is to make any impression upon them at all, and a hot-rod shop is rarely opened by someone without a known track record in the industry.

In 2002, however, this is exactly what did happen, when Hollywood Hot Rods first opened its doors in the Burbank district of Los Angeles. Troy Ladd, a young man with a business degree and a city career, had decided to swap his dark suit for t-shirt, jeans, baseball cap and a welding helmet. He was already a hot-rodder, having built his own cars at home, at one time under the stairwell of the apartment building where he lived. Enough people had said he should take up hot-rodding in earnest, but his studies and business career always got in the way. One day, the idea came into his head that if he didn't do it now, he would live to regret it.

Being well-educated and with a head for business, the first thing Troy did was to formulate a business plan, taking into

LEFT: Colourful pinstriping adorns the front door of Hollywood Hot Rods.

RIGHT: Troy Ladd, the young entrepreneur behind Hollywood Hot Rods, believes his skill and business acumen will bring success to his new venture.

OPPOSITE: A common sight: a customer's 1932 roadster sits outside Hollywood Hot Rods awaiting attention.

ABOVE & ABOVE LEFT: This 1933 five-window coupé was initially hot-rodded in the 1950s and has remained untouched ever since. Troy intends to restore it to its original 1950s specification, but with more efficient hydraulic brakes.

RIGHT: Troy fabricated these 'bomber'-style bucket seats from aluminium.

account everything needed for a successful start, such as location, size of premises, tooling etc. Troy intended to hit the ground running and to get up to speed as quickly as possible, rather than scratch a living in a back-street dive, just because the rent was cheap. Customers were paying big bucks for turn-key rods and expected certain standards; they did not frequent certain areas of Los Angeles. Therefore, Troy's choice of North Hollywood, in large premises located adjacent to the freeway and providing maximum visibility, were calculated to fit the bill. Of course, none of this would be worth much if Troy found he was unable to deliver the product. When the TV programme, RIDES, featured Troy and his crew, building a pair of Deuce roadsters for a wealthy

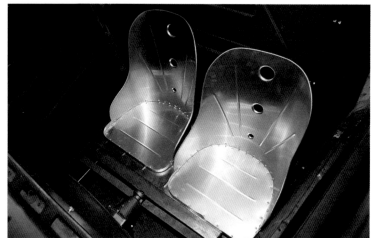

This 1932 roadster is a 1950s-built original, being restored by Hollywood Hot Rods. It has been fitted with a Cadillac V8 motor and manual transmission.

client, it was obvious to everyone that Hollywood Hot Rods was more than able to deliver the goods. No one was in any doubt that a new kid had arrived on the block, and he was taking no prisoners!

'We built a pair of '32 Hiboys in a dry-lakes style, the build was filmed for RIDES, a TV program. One's got a 400 Pontiac that was bored and stroked to 467, and it has aluminium heads that were treated to look like cast-iron heads. It's got an aluminium tri-power intake, copied from the factory cast-iron intake. The headers and the exhaust

are all hand-made to give it a dry-lakes look. It's a '32 Hiboy, it's built in a traditional way to look like a '50s/'60s vintage hot rod with bias-ply tires, which are dirt-track race tires. The chassis is a modified So-Cal and the body is a Brookville. The other car is similar, the TV program RIDES called the pair "big sister and little sister".

'I got into this thing out of necessity, my grandfather was handed down a '66 Mustang, which he gave me when I was 16. It was broke and I said – how are we going to get it going? He said, have you got any

OPPOSITE, ABOVE & RIGHT: Troy's personal rod, a 1934 Chevy three-window coupé, pictured outside his premises. The rear slick tyres are not exactly street-legal, but they are effective when Troy takes the car up the quarter-mile strip.

money? I said nope. So he said, well you better learn to fix it! So my grandfather helped me, he taught me not to be afraid, just get in and do it. Once I got into the basic mechanics of it, it was quite easy, and from there I got into the idea of going fast. I slowly learned about building it up and making it go faster and go street racing. That was about 1984. Then at a car show I saw an early hot rod and thought I'd like to build something like that, even though I didn't know what they were at the time. So then I bought a '36 Ford five-window coupé and built that when I was 19 years old.

'This here is a car we're building to show at the Grand National Show and other big events to showcase our work. It's real hard to make a '32 Ford different from what's been done before. This one is

OPPOSITE: Troy discusses how the motor is installed into the shop's latest project car.

LEFT: This 1932 roadster is being prepared for the Grand National Roadster Show, where it will showcase the work of Hollywood Hot Rods.

sectioned 2-inches lengthways, on a hand-made chassis, which is also kicked up in the rear and with a different cross member to get it lower. The wheel wells have been moved up about 5 inches in the back to match the tires. The sheetmetal has been built up around the tires. The dash is a hand-made one-off, based on a '41 Pontiac cluster. We're going to put in an injected 392 Hemi out of what was a top fuel dragster in the '50s. That will be our big thing for next year.

'The '32 over there is kind of neat, like something the Kennedy brothers might do. It's actually original, but we've had to do a lot of repair to make it right. That's an early Cadillac, tall and skinny old racing wheels. This is a '37 Chevy, found in a barn, bone stock-modern drive train, so it will be reliable. This is a '33 Ford five-window, built in the '50s – restoring it back as a '50s-built hot rod, totally traditional. It was in the guy's yard for 40 years. We'll put disc-hydraulic brakes on it – safety features. It's a survivor car, all original.

'This doesn't look like much now, it's a 1929 Ford truck, chopped, channeled and we zee'd the frame, which was hand-built. We have fitted quarter elliptical springs suspension. The springs are actually hidden in the frame rails – we try to make things different. It's got a Dodge Red Ram Hemi, it's about seven-eighths smaller than that other Hemi over there. It kind of suits this smaller car, it's in proportion. We made the frame with a lot of radius to it, a lot of round features. It's hard to do it, and it shows a high-level shop did it.

'The owner is Trevor Leen. It is a basic raw hot rod. It is going to be kind of industrial with aircraft rivets, suspension copper-plated instead of chrome. We're going to strip the paint off the car, get it to bare metal, giving a weathered rusted look – you can get green hues. It's got World War II bomber-style aircraft seats.

'The car in front of the shop with number 17 on the side is my car. It's not our shop style, it's kind of my thing, rat-roddish. I came from that Indy home-built tradition. At the car shows and speed shops the older gentlemen would kind of shoo me away or ask – where's your Dad? – did he build this car? ('36 Ford). They didn't believe that I built the whole car myself.

'I went to school and college like you're supposed to. I got a degree in business and entered the corporate world. But I always had cars on the side, and I

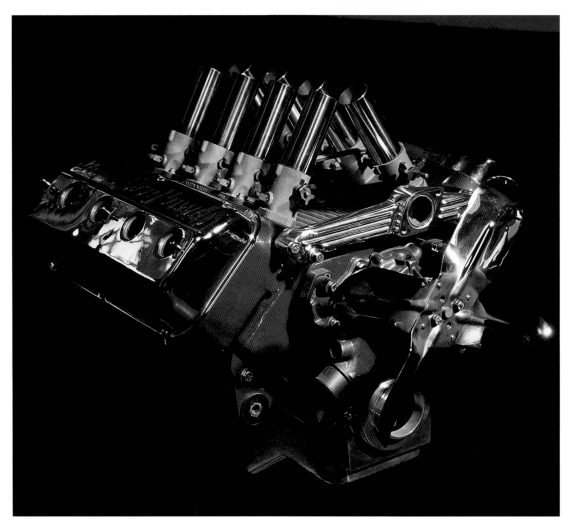

even ran a shop in a two-car garage. As time went on, I built more and more cars for me and my family members. After a while, my family said, you should open up a shop, but my attitude was no, it's my hobby, I don't want to ruin it. Later, I realized that working for someone else in the corporate world, and the stress that went with it, really cuts up, and it wasn't for me. I'm not an entrepreneur or risk-taker, so I sat down and formulated a business plan and submitted it to the bank, and when someone was offering me money, it was a choice – do I take the jump or not? So I did, and that was three years ago (2002).

'I wanted to start the shop on a larger scale, where I would hit the whole industry hard with visibility, marketing and physical size. What if you created a whole company with financial backing and a corporate image in large premises in a good area with great visibility, so that's what we did. These days hot rods are a high-dollar commodity and the clients are wealthy people who don't want to leave the car in some lot in Compton. People thought I was crazy to take on such a high-rent shop, but it's worked out. In the first two years we got coverage in 15 magazines, which was huge.

'Then there was the TV RIDES show, which gave us great exposure. I've been really lucky, I treat people well, I've got time for everyone. Now, established shops like So-Cal know who I am. Not that I consider myself competition to them – yet! Some of the biggest names are looking at what we are doing and taking notice.

'This '34 Chevy three-window coupé is my car, built in the carport of my apartment.

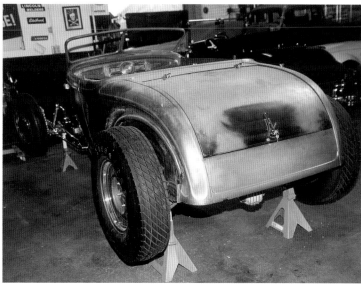

It's an original Chevy frame. I stripped it down, changed the suspension so it has the hairpin-style front, with the transverse leaf-spring kind of Ford style which looks good on a fenderless car. It's designed to look like a race car from the '50/'60s era. That's where the numbering on the side came from, and it's got the bias-ply slicks on the rear. It's got a small-block Chevy motor with a generator and pipes just like it would have been back in the '50s. It's got a 671 blower from a diesel truck, which I cut down and pieced together to fit on the Chevy block. I made a manifold to run the tri-power and the three Rochester two-barrels. I wanted a really old vintage look, and a four-barrel didn't seem to look right. So I made

that tri-power. This to me is not a rat rod – I don't really like that term, as it suggests that they are poorly built. This is a very solidly engineered car, actually. The idea behind it is the vintage old look, but it's got to be fast as well, not all for show and no go, like some of the primer cars. I race this car at the drags, at least once a year at the Antique Nationals. So it's streetable and we race it. It's a neat little car. It's as finished as it is ever going to be. Originally I built it to look weathered, but now it is really weathered. It's been very solid and reliable, and I put it together cheap, under 10 grand, real low budget.

'I chopped it and channeled it. I had to hand-build everything for it, because it's a

Chevy. It's a little bit different from all the Fords. It's actually got some nicer lines than a Ford, the back window is nicely shaped. When I chopped it, I made sure not to disrupt anything, so it's only 2½ inches out of the roof, just enough without making it obvious and unnatural-looking.

'I believe that you've got to keep proportions correct. Other people go for extreme styles, just for the sake of being extreme, for shock value. Take the truck we are currently building. We could chop a further 3 inches out of that, and it would be no higher than your waist, but to us that would be going too far, that's not our style at Hollywood Hot Rods.'

OPPOSITE: This 392 fuel-injected Hemi motor was taken from a 1950s top fuel dragster and will power the 1932 Ford show car.

ABOVE LEFT:
Where style is concerned, the Duvall windshield cannot be bettered.

ABOVE: The classic lines of the 1932 roadster are best appreciated in this rear three-quarter view.

BARRY WHITE

As is the case with many of today's leading hot-rod builders, Barry inherited his 'gearhead' tendencies from his father, who was a keen drag-racer. As a kid, Barry used to play inside the drag car, which was always being worked on in the family garage. Barry's cousins were also avid drag-racers and continue to compete to this day. It was inevitable, therefore, that Barry should follow

them into the drag-racing scene, an activity he would continue to pursue into his mid twenties, when he happened to meet some guys working on *Street Rodder* magazine. They invited Barry to help them with some project cars for the magazine, the first time he had worked on cars other than his own.

In those days, his personal car was a 1929 Ford on 1932 rails, which he sold when his daughter was born, a scenario that will be

familiar to many a hot-rodder. Usually, that would be the last one would see of that first hot rod, but for Barry, there was to be a different outcome. Over 20 years later, one of Barry's friends spotted the old car at a sale and alerted Barry to the fact. Amazingly, the car had accrued only 2,500 more miles on the clock from the time it was sold. It turns out

ABOVE: Barry and a colleague check off a list of jobs necessary to complete this project car.

LEFT: Barry White runs his Street Rod Repair Company in Corona, California.

OPPOSITE: Barry's personal 1932 roadster, resplendent in the California sunshine.

that it had ended up in Disneyland, where it was mounted on a trailer and driven by Goofy in Disney promotional events around the USA. This accounts for the lack of wear and tear on the car's chassis, but the bodywork was another matter, as way-out fenders had been fitted to make it look crazier. It was eventually auctioned off on eBay and later appeared on sale at a Long Beach swap meet, where Barry's designer, Chris, recognized it.

When Barry saw his old car he was amazed to find that, apart from beaten-up bodywork, the car was essentially the same

Barry's 1932 Ford is used on the road and the strip, hence the chromed driver's roll bars. The large billet wheels give it a 'lakester' appearance, further enhanced by the chromed push-bar on the rear. The look is finished off by the aerodynamic Duvall windshield.

as when he had built it. It had the same engine, gauges, steering-wheel – nothing was missing – so he decided to restore it exactly as it had been 20 years ago. As Barry still lives in the same house, the car now sits in the same garage as it did when Barry first

OPPOSITE: A five-window coupé with chopped roof receives a final tuning before leaving the workshop.

ABOVE LEFT: Another 1932 roadster takes shape in the Street Rod Repair Company's workshop.

ABOVE: This five-window coupé retains more traditional links, while running on billet wheels and powered by a hot Chevy motor.

LEFT: A turn-key Deuce awaits delivery to a wealthy client.

built it, so it has been a rare happy ending.

Barry continued to build project cars for *Street Rodder* magazine out of his own garage for many years, until extra work led to a need for more space, and he moved into his own professional 1,500-sq ft workshop in Newport Beach. Since then, there have been successively larger units, doubling the work area every time, until he arrived at his present 10,000-sq ft unit in Corona, California. A glance around his shop, packed with project cars, would suggest that Barry is already using the extra space to the maximum, yet surprisingly, he has only four

staff, including himself and a designer, though he maintains he needs 20. However, the high standard of work produced in Barry's shop means that suitable staff are hard to find. Consequently, everyone working must be multi-skilled and readily adaptable in order to get the job done.

A measure of the quality of Barry's output is that he received the 'America's Most Beautiful Roadster' (AMBR) award in 2001, at the Oakland roadster show, an event that has been running since 1950: it is widely recognized as one of the most prestigious awards in the industry. Barry won the ABR on his first attempt, an achievement of which he is justly proud, knowing that many big

PAGES 252 & 253: This 1932 Ford roadster, with its full-fendered style, is more a street cruiser than a racer.

PAGES 254 & 255: With its vivid flame paint scheme, this 1932 roadster creates a stunning impression on the street. The finish and detailing are faultless, while the frontal view is a perfect exercise in symmetry.

PAGES 256, 257, 258 & 259: This three-window Deuce coupé is stunning from every angle, with its flowing lines and swooping curves. The sumptuous interior puts it in a different class from the bare no-nonsense rods of the 1940s and '50s.

hitters in the hot-rod world would never be capable of such a feat. In 2003 Barry missed out on the AMBR by one point, indicating to all that his success in 2001 had been no mere fluke.

Barry's next contender for either the AMBR or the Ridler award sits under a tarpaulin, strictly off limits as far as photographers are concerned. Secrecy is paramount, as he has no wish to give the competition a clue as to how he intends to

make his roadster stand out from the pack.

His reputation is such that he is commissioned to build hot rods for very wealthy clients, who require not only a turn-key custom, but an award-winning car into the bargain. These cars are bought for keeps, being instant classics, so rarely come up for resale. However, Barry emphasizes that his cars are meant to be driven and that once the shows are over, and before the client takes delivery, he will take the key and drive the car the way it should be driven.

It is no surprise that Barry's own car is a Deuce roadster in a lakester style, right down to the push-bar on the rear. The little red roadster has a fibreglass body, bomber seats, fuel injection and bigger wheels for the salt-flat look. The driver's roll cage gives it a race-car look, but the roadster is completely street-legal, designed to be fun both on the dry lakes and the drag strip.

Barry White is undoubtedly one of the top names in the world of hot rods, and winning the AMBR award put him permanently into the hot-rod history books – an exclusive Hall of Fame. Thanks to the power of TV and the popularity of automotive reality shows on Discovery

PAGES 260, 261, 262 & 263: This checkered cab must be the ultimate taxi to hell. Its main feature is the massive supercharged Hemi engine, powering the tubbed pro-street rear wheels. It was built by Barry's SRRC for regular client, Richard Berg.

Channel, Barry's name has spread far beyond the confines of the hot-rod world and into the living rooms of the American nation.

Barry featured in a hot-rod build-off, in which he competed against Jimmy Shine. The rear of his workshop is a TV studio for about eight months of the year; at the moment a crew is filming a new show, in which Barry takes a series of project car-builds and auctions off the restored uprated vehicles.

Barry still has as much verve and

enthusiasm for hot rods that he had 20 years ago, so hopefully a steady flow of world-class cars will continue to come out of his Street Rod Repair Company. Moreover, few would take bets against his adding to his collection of industrial awards in the future.

PAGES 264, 265, 266 & 267: A purposeful-looking Deuce three-window coupé, poised for street action. With its louvred hood panels and hot flame paint job, it is impossible to ignore.

MARC & LUC DE LEY of MARCEL'S CUSTOM METAL

Entering the workshops of Marcel's Custom
Metal, one could be forgiven for thinking
one has travelled back in time, for this is a
place where the coach-building skills and
methods of the early 20th century are still
practised. Marcel's is an old-fashioned
family business, established over 30 years
ago by Marcel de Ley, and continued by his
sons, Marc and Luc, to this day. The business
of the workshop is exclusively bodywork,
where the entire skin of a car can be created
to Rolls-Royce standards, using the very
same skill and tools that manufacturers of
luxury cars employ.

Once, Marcel's concentrated solely on
luxury classic cars, and was often called
upon to replicate rare cars, such as
Duesenbergs or V12 Cadillacs. Clients would
provide a chassis and Marcel's would build a
complete body to order. The resulting
replicas were so convincing they were
indistinguishable from the real thing, and in
some cases unscrupulous owners would pass
them off as the genuine article.

Though Marcel's still works on antique
cars, it has become increasingly involved in
the hot-rod business, and some of the top
hot-rodders in the USA call upon the

RIGHT
*Luc and Marc de Ley are the craftsmen behind
Marcel's Custom Metal in Corona, California.*

*OPPOSITE: An overview of Marcel's busy
workshop.*

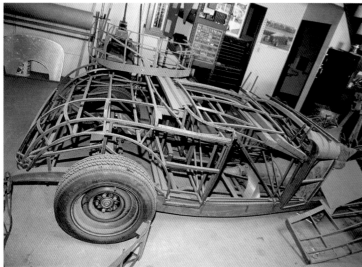

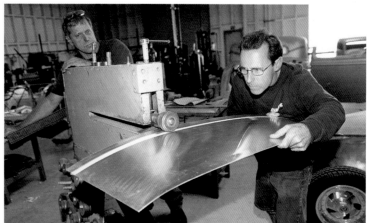

ingenuity of Marc and Luc to translate their visions from paper to metal. A method employed by the brothers is to enlarge a full-sized profile of the body design and stick it up on the workshop wall as a visual reference. They then take the chassis and create a metal skeleton reflecting the design. The skeleton is then clad in metal sheeting, using a variety of methods to shape it, such as the English wheel. In this way, a bespoke body shell is created, which is delivered to the client in bare metal form. Top builders, such as Barry White, Boyd Coddington and Chip Foose, use the de Leys' skills to translate their unique designs from paper to three-dimensional reality. It is a fact that the hot-rod world has created a demand for top-quality, high-dollar creations, and that wealthy enthusiasts are more then ready to pay for the best.

When Marcel's is asked to build a 1932 or '34 Ford show car, it recommends the car be built from scratch, based on an original body. The reason for this is that it gives the hot-rod designer more options, being unrestricted by the existing lines and form of the original. The end result may on the surface appear to be a 1932 Ford, for example, but closer scrutiny will show that it is actually only a derivative of a 1932 Ford, which incorporates designs and touches that would not have been possible given the original body shell.

Most of the work is done on a couple of

machines, including an English Wheel, which stretches and rolls the metal into the required profile, while other machines shrink the metal so that the shape of the metal panels is achieved by a skilled combination of the two processes. These are the same machines that were used on Duesenbergs and Roll-Royces in the 1920s.

Marc and Luc prefer to work on full ground-up builds, but will not accept restoration projects, accident repairs and other jobs, such as roof chops for hot rods. A typical ground-up project will take from four to six months to complete, and the brothers' reputations as craftsmen of the highest order ensure their order books are always full.

OPPOSITE ABOVE LEFT: An example of the steel skeleton on which the metal bodywork is formed.

OPPOSITE ABOVE RIGHT: Marc and Luc often work with nothing more to go by than a series of artist's impressions.

OPPOSITE BELOW: Luc forms a metal panel by passing it back and forth through an English Wheel.

RIGHT: Luc lines up a panel to assess its fit.

TONY CORREIA of HOT ROD PAINTSHOP

Hot-rodders were concerned only with performance in the early days. The sole reason for stripping down a car to create what some would call a 'gow job', was to reduce weight and increase speed and acceleration, with some adding crude flames, or maybe scallops, to their rods that had been given a matt-black coat of primer. As the scene developed and became more professional, speed shops began to create their own stylized paint schemes, So-Cal's red-and-white scallops for example, the beautiful finish achieved on its belly-tank lakesters, 1932 roadsters and coupés putting it in a class of its own. Some hot-rodders painted their cars in bright primary colours to make them stand out from the crowd.

In the 1950s and '60s, paint treatments became more elaborate, thanks to the emergence of artists such as Von Dutch, famous for his unique pinstriping and intricate flame designs. He in turn influenced future big players, such as Ed 'Big Daddy' Roth,

LEFT: Tony Correia has been in the business of painting autos for over 30 years.

OPPOSITE LEFT: Panels are meticulously wet-sanded and flattened in preparation for painting.

OPPOSITE RIGHT: having been given a coat of primer, the car awaits its turn in the paint booth.

Tony has been involved in painting hot rods for 37 years and his specialist business, Speed Shop Custom Paint (SSCP), is run in conjunction with Barry White's Street Rod Repair company. The quality of finish, needed to satisfy a customer paying possibly $150,000 for a turn-key hot rod, is understandably extremely high, and to win America's Most Beautiful Roadster, or the Ridler award, the paintwork must be flawless inside and out. Attention to detail is such that as much consideration is given to internal surfaces, not even visible, as to those that are on view, and top show judges are finding it ever more difficult to distinguish which

competitor is the most excellent. They will even use dentists' mirrors to peer into the most inaccessible corners to see if something has been missed.

It was because of this demand for perfection that Tony and Barry created SSCP, so establishing control of all stages in the painting process, while at the same time removing themselves from the uncertainties of using outside paint shops. Consequently, Tony is constantly drumming into his staff the need for attention to detail. Quality control is everything, and should he consider the workmanship not quite up to scratch, he will have no qualms but to have the car stripped

who not only painted cars, but also began to build concept custom cars from the ground up. The psychedelic visions of Ed Roth and his peers during the 1960s gave rise to a more competitive custom scene, not necessarily related to dry-lakes racing.

Increasingly, drag racing became the choice of racers and race-goers, while on abandoned ex-Second World War airfields in California, a burgeoning drag-racing scene had developed, where races took place every night of the week. The rise in sponsorship also created a demand for ever more intricate and imaginative ideas, which swiftly became a prerequisite of success in custom car competitions and shows in general.

Consequently, as many paint shops as speed shops sprang into existence, and a career in creative painting was suddenly an option for many.

Today, many of the materials and methods used even 20 years ago have been outlawed on grounds of health or pollution. The lacquer-based paints, once universally used, are now banned in most states, and the day of the back-street painter has long since gone. Regulations now demand that a professional paintshop be equipped with paint booths costing hundreds of thousands of dollars, and just such an operation can be found in Corona, California, run by veteran painter, Tony Correia.

down and the process begun again. Tony is
aware his criticisms hurt his employees'
feelings, but wants them to know that good
enough is far from perfect, and if they can't
accept this important fact they are of no
further use.

Tony knows his business inside out, and
his greatest reward is seeing the look of
delight on customers' faces when they take
delivery of their car, a car they may well have
dreamed of owning for many years; it is at
this moment that all the hours of painstaking
work seem justified. After all, it is the car's
surface one initially sees, then its lines, then
all the design features a builder like Barry
White has incorporated into his creation. It
doesn't matter how clever the design – this
can be completely spoiled by less than perfect
paintwork.

Tony employs five other people at SSCP.
He has a specialist responsible for working on
fibreglass hot rods and Corvettes, and an
expert metalworker, while others
painstakingly prepare the panels for painting.
Priming and sanding-down are among the
least glamorous jobs, but they are as important
as any other stage in the building process, and
a perfect finish can only be applied to a
perfectly-prepared surface. Tony, incidentally,
considers his painters to be the best in the
business.

Painting techniques have changed over
the years: now, gravity feed guns are used to
apply the paint, and since lacquer-based paints
were outlawed in California, it has been found
that the eurethane and acrylic paints are not as
easy to apply. A 'nine-mile deep' effect can
be achieved using a process of rubbing-down

and shining-up many layers of paint, when the illusion is created that one can dip one's hand right in.

Tony describes how a typical paint job is done at SSCP. First, three coats of primer are applied and sanded down, using ever finer sand blocks, after which the surface is ready for the first coat of paint. Then a clear coat is sprayed over that and sanded down, and then the flames go on, sprayed over with another clear coat and again sanded down. The pinstriping is then applied and a last clear coat is followed by a final sanding. The flames and pinstriping are applied by outside specialist Phil Whetstone, who has a reputation as one of the best in the business. SSCP's order books are full to overflowing, and the staff regularly work 12- to 14-hour days to ensure jobs are completed.

It is common for engines to be painted to match the bodywork. For this, the same paint is used, as it can withstand the 180–200-degree heat generated by the engine. Once again, the secret here is painstaking preparation, as a motor and transmission have endless nooks and crannies needing to be

rubbed-down and evenly sprayed. A car is judged on every aspect of the building process, including what is beneath the hood.

The paint booth installed at SSCP is a

down-draft system, costing around $100,000 and made by Sprayzone. It is the 'Çadillac' of spray booths and certainly delivers the necessary results. Tony ordered the system

with the highest specification to make sure the company was complying with local regulations, which are among the most stringent in the USA.

OPPOSITE: This body is almost ready to go back to the SSCP workshop and be fitted back onto its chassis.

RIGHT: After pinstriping the flames, this car is further block-sanded, when a further clear coat will be applied in the Sprayzone booth.

ROBERT WILLIAMS

Robert Williams was into hot rods from an early age, and claims to have driven a 1934 Ford five-window coupé when he was 12 years old. He had a couple of buddies who shared his love of hot-rodding and they were responsible for building some of the most dangerous rods on the road. People were not as concerned with safety in those days, and sometimes the modifications that were attempted exceeded the mechanical skills of the young mechanics. Williams describes how they regularly went on forays into the countryside, looking for old abandoned cars from which they could scavenge parts. Sometimes these expeditions bordered on theft, as no great efforts were made to trace the owners of the parts they took: occasionally they were caught by the local sheriff, who suggested a form of reparation be offered. In spite of this, Williams' garage was soon stuffed to the rafters with 1923 Ford roadster bodies, chassis and other automotive paraphernalia.

By 1959 Robert Williams was in high school and an avid reader of auto magazines, such as *Hop Up*, *Hot Rod*, *Car Craft* and *Rod & Custom*. These were only just beginning to feature the work of hot-rod artists and builders such as Von Dutch and Ed 'Big

RIGHT: Artist Robert Williams, at home with his pair of Deuces.

OPPOSITE: Robert Williams used to drive this 1932 primer roadster – called Aces and Eights.

Daddy' Roth. In addition to his interest in mechanics, Williams also had an artistic bent and was deeply influenced by the way Von Dutch and Roth applied their artistic talents in the hot-rod world.

Von Dutch revolutionized the world of customizing with his unique brand of pinstriping, and while flame decoration on cars was not new, it was usually amateurish and lacking in depth when tackled by a non-expert. The way Von Dutch painted flames was a cut above the others; he liked to finish off the realistic licking flames by applying expert pinstriping.

Big Daddy Roth was heavily influenced by Von Dutch's work and was no mere amateur himself. Moreover, Roth was a hot-rodder with a unique style of his own and

was not a follower of established trends. He was also a great cartoonist, having invented monstrous characters, such as Rat Fink,

ABOVE: A simple dashboard is decorated with pinstriping.

ABOVE RIGHT: Robert Williams favours a rumble seat over the trunk space.

RIGHT: These graphics were painted by Robert himself.

OPPOSITE: The roadster is powered by a 350 Chevy motor.

PAGES 280 & 281: The roadster's paint job is intended to make it look like an old race car.

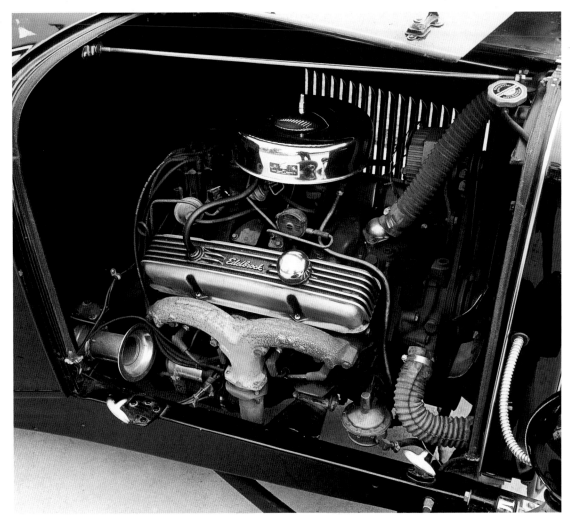

OPPOSITE & LEFT: Robert's Deuce coupé is also powered by a Chevy 350: Robert refers to it as his 'winter car'.

which became instantly popular with hot-rodders and surfers.

These men were gods as far as Robert Williams was concerned and the Californian scene was too attractive not to experience it for himself. So Robert inevitably found himself in Los Angeles, which was the hub of car-culture as well as counter-cultures of all types.

After a stint at art school, Robert heard that Roth was looking for an artist to work with him at his Maywood studio and he was fortunate to land the job. By now it was the mid 1960s and Robert was suddenly not only involved with Ed Roth but also with Von Dutch and other underground artists involved in producing subversive images. The laid-back Bohemian atmosphere suited Robert well and he found himself fitting into a scene in which new t-shirt designs and comic-book graphics and cartoons were being produced. These included advertisements executed as monochrome pen-and-ink sketches, often highly detailed and darkly humorous. This was a perfect training ground for Robert, who would go on to produce ground-breaking and possibly law-breaking underground comics, such as *Zap*, the fourth issue of which ended up the subject of criminal court proceedings in New York, and was declared obscene by the judge.

Just as hot-rodders challenged mainstream cars, so the cartoon and comic-book artists pushed back barriers and

offended the easily shocked. As a hot-rodder and underground artist, Robert Williams was combining aspects of the two scenes in the art he produced and the cars he drove, such as his Eights & Aces Deuce roadster. Both he and his wife Suzanne, who has a 1934 Ford sedan, favour the unfinished look reminiscent of the old-school rods of the 1940s. They were among the first to revive this 'look', inspiring the present-day craze for rat rods that are so popular with the younger rockabilly crowd today.

Over the years Robert has produced a string of beautifully-detailed oil paintings, which also demonstrate his perfect understanding and experience of the mechanics of hot rods, and which also

include characters pioneered by his mentor, Ed Roth. Arguably his best-known work is the 1976 acrylic on board, *Hot Rod Race*, which depicts a bunch of rodders being pursued by the law, while a collision is happening to the side. The 1988 *Snuff Fink* depicts a couple in a purple roadster, the blonde female seemingly terrified by a vision of a grotesque multi-eyeballed monster abusing itself with knives, drugs, guns and glue, while being transported by an equally monstrous five-window coupé. Hallucinatory visions of hot-rod accidents and monstrous characters also appear in work such as Death on the Boards (1991) and *A White-Knuckle Ride for Lucky St Christopher*.

Today, Robert Williams is recognized as

an important American artist. His New York exhibitions are always sell-outs, and his work is avidly collected. Hot-rodding is still close to his heart, and a 1932 roadster and a coupé sit in his garage alongside Suzanne's sedan and classis Ford Thunderbird. Suzanne, an artist in her own right, is also a confirmed 'gearhead' and together they still attend hot-rod gatherings such as the Primer Nationals in Ventura, California.

Robert was interviewed in September 2005, when he discussed Von Dutch, Ed Roth, his art and his hot rods at his home and studio in North Hollywood.

'Well, this here is my '32 Ford roadster. I bought the body in 1968 for $200 when I was art director at Roth Studios. Jim Jacobs

found it for me. I had been looking for a nice roadster body for a long, long time – good ones are hard to find. Jim used to work at Roth's studio and I asked him if he could find me a '32 roadster body – I don't want a coupé with the top sawed off, and I don't want a cabriolet. He said – get your checkbook, I've found one for you. We went out to Seal Beach and for 200 bucks I got this body and I also got a frame, rear end, steering, that radiator shell and radiator, the seat cushions and a pink slip, so immediately I registered this pile of junk and searched for

ABOVE & OPPOSITE: The coupé has a sumptuous leather interior; note the headliner detail. It also has a rumble seat.

284

*OPPOSITE: Suzanne Williams has had her 1934
Ford sedan since 1973 and prefers the matt-
painted look.*

*LEFT: The 1934 sedan has a beautiful roof chop,
retaining all the fluidity of the swage lines.*

parts at swap meets and picked up a little bit here and a little bit there.

'Now let me, if I may, make a profoundly conceited remark about this car. This car was put together and running when Pete Eastwood worked at Pete & Jakes, with Pete Chapouris and Jim 'Jake' Jacobs. They said – we'll help you assemble this car, we'll put this car together for you and straighten that chassis, but we want to make sure that this car is never painted, so that we will know that there is always one primer '32 roadster on the streets. So this was the first primer car that was predicated finished back in the late '70s, early '80s. This was the forerunner of those cars that were at the Primer Nationals in Ventura. Right after this, Pete Eastwood was on the cover of *Hot Rod* magazine with a '32 two-door sedan that was a primer. It was the first such car to get on the cover of *Hot Rod* magazine. No one before had declared a primer car as finished – that's it, that's the direction I intended to go – I'm there! Well I drove this car more than 20 years in primer, and I was absorbed by this whole young society in primer, and I found myself a prisoner of this thing. I decided that I wanted color, with a really rambunctious lurid old race-car paint job on it. So I painted it the color that they painted stock cars and dragsters back in the '50s with this design that violates the lines of the car. As a kid I hated this kind of paint job, which had no consideration for the lines of the car, but it looked really good from the grandstands of the racetrack or dragstrip. So I thought, well this is the right way to do it. So I got a body man to work out all the body problems and I drew out all the designs on tracing paper and transferred it to the car. I had painted the cartoons on the back, and I got a lettering artist to gold-leaf the numbers and stripe it for me. Sometimes I come into the garage and think, man, what an eyesore, but it's right. If you take the top off, remove the windshield and fenders, this thing all of a sudden just pops! The reality of what it is, a race car, really stands out. When you take off the headlights, and break it down to its racing essentials, all of a sudden it looks aggressive.

'Now the '32 three-window coupé. I've got the fenders, running-board and bumpers for it. The body came out of San Diego, I was told that it was chopped in '52. It had been though a bunch of hands, it was a gutted shell, an old race-car shell, and it needed an enormous amount of work doing

to it. The top was chopped two-and-three-quarter-inches and I thought, that's an odd amount, I would have chopped it three or three-and-a-half inches myself. Some older guys told me that this was called a 'beauty chop', back in the '50s. The reason they didn't chop it to three inches was because to run on the dry lakes, you'd be put into competition class, but this way it could be run in street class. Both of these cars have 350 Chevys, the roadster has a four-speed in it and this one's got an automatic. The coupé's my bad-weather car and the roadster is my sports car.

'My wife Suzanne has her own rod, a

'34 sedan – had it since '73. We chopped it in '88, it's got a Chevy with a four-speed, which we put in in '95. We then painted it all one-color primer and had everything rechromed. This sedan has a remarkable interior in it. It's a very fast car and has had a beautiful chop job done to it. The windshields have been leaned back, the top's been moved forward, it doesn't have fillers in the center. It's got a real aerodynamic look to it. The car was exceptionally well-preserved when Suzanne got it in '73. The fenders have never been off the car, they had been loosened up and had weld stripped in. The car has never been in a collision. It was

a drag car at one time, it had a full race 283 in it. It had chrome rings that didn't seat. We got rid of that engine. Suzanne used to sit up way on high like in a gas coupé. She had Pete Eastwood put a drop axle in it.

'Art and hot rods came to my interest at about the same time – my adolescence I guess. I got my first car at age 12, it was a '34 Ford five-window coupé in Alabama. My father owned stock cars in the south. He ran around dirt tracks in the '50s. I've always been around old Fords, old square-top Fords – I developed a real thing for them. In the early '50s I ran across *Hot Rod* magazine and I realized that there was a whole culture

of people who were into old Fords and I got real involved in hot rods. I had that old '34 Ford and there followed one junky Ford after another.

'By chance, I ended up working with Ed Roth as his art director. A lot of very talented people passed through Ed's studio. It was a very interesting place to work. I was already involved with underground comics like *Zap*, working with people like Robert Crumb and other psychedelic artists, so when Ed closed the studio down in 1970, I just carried on with the comics and my personal painting. I haven't had a boss since 1970.

'The hot rod world is different from the

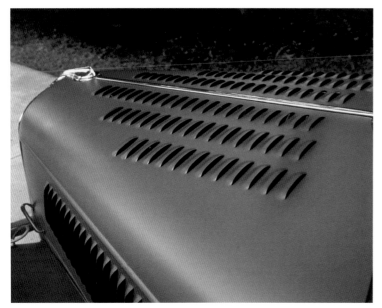

motorcycle world. It's not so easy to get into it because you've got to go out and find and build something, no-one's going to hand you anything. When you buy a turn-key car, it's going to cost $80–100,000. Original cars are at a premium now, they're so expensive, ridiculously expensive.

'The art of pinstriping vehicles probably goes back hundreds of thousands of years. The act of dragging a brush along a straight line to decorate a stagecoach or chariot is a very old art. Von Dutch was the first person to get all psychotic with pinstriping. Von Dutch told me that the reason he got into that was because someone brought him a vehicle

which had grinder or sander marks under the paint. So Von Dutch pinstriped some swirls to disguise the sanding marks. He then made corresponding swirls to achieve a symmetry. Von Dutch liked how it looked, and so did the owner, so Von Dutch continued to develop this new way of decorating cars, and he just got more psychotic on it. Well, Von Dutch was a little psychotic to begin with, so it suited him perfectly. He was also one of the prime instigators of flames – he didn't invent flames but he was the first person to bring flames to the forefront. There had been flames on aircraft and race cars back in the '20s and '30s, but they were crude and

goofy-looking. Von Dutch was the first to do those moving, romantic rhythmic flames.

'Von Dutch was a very interesting person, he was a friend of ours at one time, he was tremendously inspirational to Roth. Roth styled himself completely on Von Dutch. Von Dutch as a person was kind of an asshole, he was really a jerk, very right and bigoted. But you find that among the motorcycle crowd (Von Dutch was very into motorcycles). You find that amongst the hot-rod crowd, to a certain extent, because they're mechanical people. Before Von Dutch died, he was very ill with liver problems, he wrote this horrible letter condemning

mankind and all the minorities and the Jews, etc, and he openly admitted that he was a Nazi, even though the Nationalist Socialist Party would have nothing to do with someone like him. He would have been amongst the first to be shipped out to a concentration camp. Anyway, this letter

ABOVE & OPPOSITE: The sedan has a fine two-tone leather interior, complete with matching booster seat for the diminutive Suzanne. The hood and side panels are enhanced by louvres.

PAGES 290 & 291: Examples of Robert's paintings – Hot Rod Race and Snuff Fink.

floated around for about a decade and I kept waiting for it to surface and it finally did in the *LA Times*. This was quite an embarrassment to the company currently selling Von Dutch-branded fashion to liberal left-wing fashionistas. A TV company came to interview me to see what my take on this letter was. I explained to them – you know Blackbeard the pirate left quite an interesting beautiful romantic legacy, but you wouldn't have wanted to run around with the guy! Von Dutch was a tremendous influence on me and thousands of young people, but politically he was a screwball, he was a tyrant. I kind of tried to help his image but there was no helping it. A lot of people who wear the Von Dutch branded gear don't know who he was – I heard someone say they thought he was some gay clothes designer! Von Dutch hated commerce, and he hated money. This exploitation of his name is completely contradictory to his direction of life. Someone called me from New York to get my take on this commercialization of Von Dutch's name and I said – can you hear that? They said, hear what? Von Dutch, turning over in his grave – spinning!

'A black guy who discovered that Von Dutch was a racist said to me – what do you think about this, I'm wearing this Von Dutch gear? Well, I said – you know the sonofabitch threatened to kill me – but I still wear a Von Dutch shirt because he was such a romantic asshole.

'He didn't have Tourette's syndrome, but he had a reactionary way when he would outburst on people. If he went into a

crowd, especially bikers – he hated bikers, thought they were pretentious – he'd go to a biker bar and he'd stand up on the bar, and he would tell them how asinine they looked in their biker costumes, that they were all phonies. Then someone would jerk him off of the bar and beat the crap out of him. He would get a good beating a couple of times a year. He was very dangerous as he either had a gun on him or he was in reach of a pistol, and he had shot people. He wasn't someone to toy with. He had a rich sense of humour, but it was a right-wing sense of humour.

'He was so mechanically-inclined – he was a critical mass of interesting mechanical facts. We'd stay up all night, drinking Foster's beer and discussing mechanical philosophy. I'd ask him questions like – on a World War I aeroplane engine, which turned, how did the motors get gas? – and he'd know. Any facts or details about a firearm or anything else he would know, he had a photographic memory for instruction manuals and such like.

'He had a crazy huge ego, he would have no problem telling you that he was the next Da Vinci. Ed Roth came along and saw

all his qualities. Von Dutch set down the path and we all followed it. Ed Roth and Von Dutch got on together very very well, but Dutch would make snide remarks about Roth, like all the things that Roth had done ought to be put in a pile and set on fire. He wouldn't say those things to Ed's face. Ed worshipped him – even when Ed got religious in his later years, he would still defend that sonofabitch.'

ABOVE: Robert and Suzanne Williams.

OPPOSITE: Robert in his studio.

ED 'BIG DADDY' ROTH

California was a unique place after the Second World War – a kind of creative primeval soup that spawned a whole range of sub-cultures, many of which spread across the globe. Motorcycle gangs, hot-rodders, surfers, beatnik poets, Latino lowriders – they were all there, plus a generation of free-thinkers and anti-establishment types – they were all part of the swinging sixties, with its free love, hippies, drug culture and rock music.

Ed Roth was born in Beverly Hills, California in 1932. His father, a German-speaking cabinet-maker, was a man accustomed to using his hands, and he taught Ed to do the same. By the age of 14, Ed was already the owner of a 1933 Ford coupé, which he drove to high school by day and went street-racing and cruising in it at night. After graduating, he went to college to study engineering, hoping to learn more about car design, but he abandoned his studies after two years and signed up with the air force in 1951, where he learned to be a cartographer.

He stayed in the military for four years, then, having acquired a wife and five sons, he worked for the Sears department store as a designer in the display department, but even so found it difficult to make ends meet; to feed his large family, he began to paint and stripe cars in the evenings after work.

Ed Roth's creative life really started when he joined forces with Bud Crozier, also known as The Baron. They opened up a shop in Southgate together, called Baron & Roth, where they designed crazy t-shirts, and painted flames, scallops and pinstriping on hot-rod cars. Roth, who had always been

interested in auto-engineering, then began to build rods of his own.

The first of these was like no other in existence, being a one-off creation, a mobile sculpted work of art in metal and fibreglass. Completed in 1959, Roth called it The Outlaw, and it certainly caused a stir: he appeared to be one of the first to apply psychedelic art to cars. Roth continued to build one special car each year, each different from the last. The Beatnik Bandit, Road Agent, Orbitron, Roatar, Surfite and Mysterian were some of the most famous,

and some looked like something out of a Jetson cartoon, their perspex dome-covered cockpits being quite unsuitable for the Californian climate. However, they were not built to be functional – they were simply to

OPPOSITE: From left to right, Robert Williams, Ed Roth and Von Dutch. (Photo by Suzanne Williams.)

ABOVE: Ed 'Big Daddy' Roth airbrushes a t-shirt.

LEFT: A cover of Car Craft magazine featuring Beatnik Bandit – a typical Roth creation.

advertise his prospering t-shirt business.

Roth was one of the first artists to airbrush unique designs onto t-shirts, and in the process developed a host of grotesque and monstrous characters, often depicted either surfing or driving grossly-exaggerated hot-rod cars.

OPPOSITE: The Outlaw of 1959 was the first of a long line of one-off Roth creations. The decoration is an example of 1950s psychedelia.

ABOVE: Side Walk Surfer – one of the monstrous characters created by Roth.

RIGHT: Roth's best-known creation – Rat Fink.

The king of these, and probably the best-known, is Rat Fink, a demonic, psychotic rat, supported by a bizarre band of 'finks' – Surfink, Angel Fink, Boss Fink (Roth himself), and Superfink. They were equally beloved of hot-rodders and surfers and were the basis of a series of Monster Kits made by Revell. The cars and monster kits produced in the 1960s were significant money-spinners for Roth: it is said that in 1962 Revell paid a royalty to him of a cent per kit sold: that year, Roth made $32,000 in royalties, which amply demonstrates the popularity of Roth's cars and creations with young people all over the world.

It is fair to say that Ed Roth enjoyed worldwide fame as a result of his creations, but he was also seen by some as a subversive figure, against the backdrop of the 1960s hippie peacenik movement. Certainly, many of his monsters seemed to have lost contact with external reality, having bulging bloodshot eyeballs and long, dribbling dangling tongues. *Time* magazine described Roth as 'Supply Sergeant to the Hell's Angels'.

To Roth, however, it was all about having fun. By now, he had taken to wearing a tuxedo with top hat and monocle, when appearing in public, after he had been criticized for looking too scruffy in his trademark t-shirts. With his beatnik goatee beard, he certainly bore a distinct resemblance to Salvador Dali.

In the late 1960s Roth turned his attention to trikes, three-wheeled vehicles that were neither car nor bike, which caused him to be shunned by the hot-rod/custom-car world, which outlawed these creations from their shows, though they were viewed a little more kindly by the customizers.

In 1970 Big Daddy Roth closed down his studio, which had employed several artists: one of these, who worked for Roth between 1965 and 1970, was Robert Williams, a hot-rodder and anti-establishment artist, who would go on to make a huge contribution to custom culture in later years.

Roth, meanwhile, dropped out for a few years, and it is said that he hung out during this time with outlaw motorcycle gangs in the California desert. He was later to return, and in the late 1970s and early '80s was again building trikes such as Asphalt Angel and the Globe Hopper.

Roth was intrigued by smaller, more energy-efficient vehicles and later, after moving to Utah, became interested in designing solar-powered vehicles. His ambition was to build a 200-mpg rod, which was quite a revolutionary idea at the time, but totally in keeping with today's environmentally-aware attitudes.

Roth continued to build strange one-off creations, such as a child's buggy, powered by a lawn-mower engine, called the Conestoga Star in 1992. In fact, hot-rodding enjoyed a revival in the 1990s, and this reignited interest in the artistic and cultural significance of Roth's body of work. Big Daddy, however, refused to take himself too seriously. He once said, 'I was just a guy trying whatever wild thought popped into my mind – I never spent any time thinking about art, I just did things.' Sadly, Big Daddy passed away in April 2001, leaving a new generation of finks to carry on in his absence.

Road Agent was one of the many Roth vehicles immortalized in Revell's model kits.

298

BOYD CODDINGTON

Boyd Coddington is one of the most important hot-rod builders alive today. The TV show, American Hot Rod, shown on the Discovery Channel, has managed to bring all the ups and downs associated with building a hot rod into the living rooms of the public at large, and has turned viewers with no particular interest in custom cars into aficionados.

Boyd's reputation as one of the most innovative hot-rodders in the world was not easily earned. As is the case with many famous names in the business, he was fascinated by automobiles from an early age. He grew up as a farm boy in rural Idaho, and would have had more than a passing acquaintance with things mechanical. Every farm boy needs to know how to keep the old tractor or pickup running, so repairs and maintenance would have been second nature, as would using any materials that came to hand. At the age of 13, Boyd traded in his shotgun for a 1931 Chevy pickup truck and so began his interest in cars and modifying them that would eventually make him a household name in the hot-rod world.

Boyd later trained as a machinist and served a three-year apprenticeship, while in his spare time he chopped and changed a variety of cars, while avidly consuming all the hot-rod magazines he could lay his hands on. It would have been the influence of these magazines that led him out of the rural void

Boyd Coddington, probably the most high-profile hot-rod builder in the world.

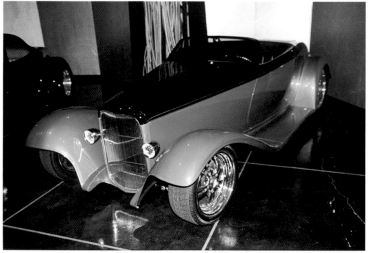

In 1981, a Boyd Coddington-built 1933 Ford coupé won the Al Slonaker award at the Oakland Roadster Show. Boyd then went on to win an unprecedented and unequalled seven America's Most Beautiful Roadster Awards (AMBR) at the Grand National Roadster Show. By now, his reputation was such that he was the builder of choice for stars such as Billy Gibbons of ZZ Top, for whom he built Cadzilla.

By the 1990s, Boyd was known as the King of Billet: the advent of CNC machines now meant that the mass-production of computer-designed aluminium billet parts was within the reach of all. Boyd embraced this relatively new technology and as a result, his hot rods were now smooth seamless designs with many billet details, and eventually billet wheels. In fact, Boyd's commercial success was based on these, which sold at the rate of over 100,000 per year.

Boyd became a member of the SEMA Hall of Fame in 1995. In 1996, in conjunction with Chip Foose, he developed the Boydster, which was built for drummer Michael Anthony of the rock group, Van Halen. The basis of Boydster I was the 1932 Highboy roadster: the body was hand-crafted in steel and the hood in aluminium, while 1934 'suicide' doors were fitted and the interior was lavishly upholstered in red leather to match the exterior paintwork. The car won yet another AMBR award. Boyd then created a fibreglass kit whereby anyone could order a Boydster and build one for themselves.

Today, Boyd Coddington Hot Rods

OPPOSITE : Boyd pictured with a Model A pickup (left) and a pair of show-winning Boydsters: the two-tone car was an AMBR winner.

BELOW: Boyd built this five-window coupé for the actor Nicolas Cage.

occupies a massive 50,000-sq ft (4645-m²) workshop and showroom. Boyd runs the operation together with his wife and ex-wife. His workshop manager, Duane, handles the day-to-day problems of running the business with all the attack of a rabid dog, but with less finesse. All of this is brought to the public gaze by Discovery Channel's Friday-night show, American Hot Rod, which chronicles the trials and tribulations of completing a project from the ground up, usually working to impossible deadlines. Every week, Boyd's employees become stressed, exhausted, and usually thoroughly exasperated, due to the crazy demands made of them by Boyd and Duane. The show is now compulsive viewing for many, because of the human drama that unfolds (some of which may be contrived), as the crew works day and night to finish on time.

Boyd comes across as a hard taskmaster, who seems genuinely surprised when one of his beleaguered staff downs tools and heads for pastures new, and surprise quickly turns to ire if the new pastures include working for his bête noir, Chip Foose, with whom he appears to have unfinished business.

Boyd may be a controversial figure, if the TV show is to be believed, but nevertheless, his record speaks for itself. No

and into the exciting and glamorous world of Californian hot-rodding. At that time California was seen as a promised land, where anyone seeking their fortune was bound to succeed: it was also the place where hot-rodding began, before spreading like wildfire to the rest of the world.

In 1966, at the age of 22, Boyd made the

move to California, where he worked as a machinist for a company called Western Gear, and built hot rods in his spare time. During the 1970s, Boyd gained a reputation for building great hot rods, until 1978, when he made the big leap forward and opened a hot-rod shop, initially sited in the garage behind his house in Cypress, California.

one else can boast seven AMBR awards, and as Boyd himself points out, his business puts food on the table for 70 families.

CHIP FOOSE

Is artistic ability inherited – part of a person's genome – or does it depend on environmental influences? The argument nature or nurture, or whether development is a combination of the two, has raged for decades. Where Chip Foose is concerned, however, a healthy dose of both were in evidence from the beginning. The son of hot-rod builder and designer, Sam Foose, Chip was allowed into the design studio of AMT, a manufacturer of model cars, when he was between one and three years old. There, his father, Sam, designed to-scale models of hot rods in conjunction with Gene Winfield, another ground-breaking designer, so Chip must have been nurtured in what amounted to a hothouse of creativity.

His father eventually moved on to a company called Minicars, where his task was to develop safety features for car prototypes, funded by the government: needless to say – where Sam went Chip went too. Incredibly, at the age of seven, Chip joined his father's company – Project Design – where he began painting car bodies. He also learned to draw the prototype vehicles built by the company, after copying his father's technique and designs. Later, former Ford and Tucker designer, Alex Tremulis, came across the talented young Foose, and recognizing something very special in the youngster, suggested he attend art school.

As a result, Chip went to study art, but

was soon in financial difficulties and had to leave after two years and go to work for a living. He again joined his father, illustrated magazines and took on freelance work for a small technical-design company, that was later to become ASHA, in Santa Barbara. There he worked on developing new technical solutions to problems related to the automotive industry. It was at ASHA that he also made clay models and built car bodies. Even more important, he learned to translate his ideas into drawings.

With ASHA's backing, Chip returned to school and completed his degree. He became involved with Boyd Coddington around that time, building hot rods and show cars, even though he had been invited to join Ford's design team. He designed the Boydster during his time at Coddington's, and was responsible for two AMBR awards. Unfortunately, Coddington's encountered financial difficulties and Chip had no choice but to strike out on his own. The timing could not have been worse, his wife Lynne was pregnant, and he had less than $1,000 in the bank. Many would have despaired under the circumstances, but Chip Foose always believed in the power of positive thinking. He was rewarded a week later with a lucrative design contract from the audio company, Precision Power, and thus Foose Design was born.

Perhaps it is because Chip knows what it is to live under financial pressure, that he prefers to keep his company small and simple. He seems genuinely able to relate to people from all walks of life, though he has a reputation as a workaholic and is not afraid

to get oil on his hands, should the occasion arise. Chip's reputation as a highly-talented and innovative automotive designer is not only recognized by many in the mainstream automotive industry, but also in the world of hot rods and custom cars. He was described by Chris Bangle, chief of design at BMW, as one of the most important and influential designers in the world today, which is quite a tribute.

With his 1935 Chevrolet and a 1934 Ford three-window coupé, Chip won the coveted Ridler award at the Detroit Autorama on two consecutive occasions, in 2002 and 2003, which is considered by many to be the ultimate achievement. Successive wins had never been achieved by any other builder since the inception of the awards in 1964. In 2005 Foose Design did it again with a 1936 Ford roadster, built for a client, Ken Reister.

For such a successful designer and builder, Chip seems creditably modest and down-to-earth. He collaborates with many other top builders, such as Troy Trepanier, and does not often attach his name to such projects. Similarly, he works as a consultant in the mainstream automotive industry, but declines to discuss the fact – a rare attribute in an egocentric world.

Thanks to Discovery Channel's show, Overhaulin', the public at large now has an insight into the way the great man works. The format of the show involves 'stealing' the car of an unsuspecting member of the public in collaboration with the victim's friends and family. The car – usually a junk heap, with only sentimental value, is passed on to the Foose team, who have a week to

transform it into a dream car, while meanwhile the Discovery presenters bamboozle the victim with fake police interviews and humorous scenarios.

Foose begins the overhaul by sketching out his ideas for the transformation in felt-tip pen, which is the method he always uses, whatever the project. The team then works flat out for 24 hours a day to achieve the seemingly impossible, and it does not go unnoticed that Chip stays with the project all the way, at times snatching a few hours' sleep on the workshop floor. This is no TV sham, and Chip's often haggard looks and baggy eyes are patently not the product of the make-up studio.

Chip Foose seems to have a burning desire to get as much done as is humanly possible, and he often takes on crazy schedules, balancing them against his services to industry, his TV commitments, and running what may be the best hot-rod shop in the world.

MIKE PARTI

The huge surge of nostalgia for the 1940s and '50s has transformed the hot-rod scene, returning at least a part of it to the young and not so wealthy enthusiast. The 'rat-rodder' scene is now flourishing, as today's young 'greasers' try to recreate the cars driven at the dry lakes before and after the Second World War. These cars were not pretty, in fact they were often quite ugly: the body was left totally unfinished, or at best given a prime coat and left at that.

In those days, power and performance were more important than appearance. Custom car shows, where style and glitz were paramount, had yet to be developed, and what money there was went to buy more horsepower, rather than paint, the only aim being to have a good time on the dry lakes or a win at the drags. This is the old-school attitude that young rat-rodders nowadays seem to be emulating, along with the hair styles, clothes and music of the time.

Mike Parti drives a rat rod, a 1927 Model T chassis with a narrowed T bucket body, which he built himself to drag-race. Mike, however, is no slavish follower of fashion, he is the real deal, a hot-rodder of the true old school, because he was doing it the first time around in the 1950s. Mike is not a young rat-rodder, he is very nearly a septuagenarian and is still enjoying hot-rodding. He still goes to rat-rod events and is

Mike Parti has been a hot-rodder since the 1950s. He is pictured here in his garage with his 1934 coupé.

welcomed by the younger crowd, many of whom recognize the genuine article when they see it. Mike is well-respected because he knows how it was done in those days, there being no text books or manuals to explain the difference between the right way and the wrong way. As Mike sees it, there are many options, where motor set-up, carburettor and intake combinations, gear ratios, transmissions and ignition systems are concerned. He knows which combinations worked on a 1927 Ford or a 1932 roadster, because he grew up with them. As he says, 'In those days you were always broke, greasy and dirty if you were a hot-rodder. We all worked on our own cars and helped each other. Most of us raced drags, dry lakes or jalopies. We used to street-race too, but it

was not the heavy deal like the Japanese cars of today. There was a lot of open country round here in those days, believe it or not. There wasn't too much to hit if you crashed. Of course it's all built-up now. In those days we went to Inglewood or Culver City, those were the hotbeds of hot-rodding. We went to Stan's drive-in, Teddy's and Bob's, which is still going big-time today. One good thing, there were a lot of girls attracted to hot rods for some reason. It couldn't have been money, 'cos we were all broke all the time. In the early '50s I was in high school and my girlfriend would walk down to my house, where I was tinkering with some car – all dirty. I used to earn 25 cents an hour as a grease monkey, and a date consisted of driving around, going to some drive-in café. Two cokes and a shared portion of French fries was all I could afford, so those girls must have liked cars, or they liked the fact that most hot-rodders were perceived as hoodlums by straight society or something. It's a little bit the same way today where all these young rat-rodders are concerned. They dress like we used to, they grease their hair into DAs, they sure got more tattoos than we did though, as it was frowned upon in the '50s. Some of the high-dollar hot-rodders who have got into it, since they got successful, kind of sneer at these kids in their rusty old buckets and primer jobs. I don't like that. I tell them I don't agree. These kids are talking the talk and walking the walk, just like back in the day, and they're building their own stuff in back yards just like we used to. Hell, get used to it, it's all going to be their scene when we're gone, that's for

sure. No, I got a lot of time for them, they treat me nice and respectful, and I go to a lot of their get-togethers.

'As well as my '27 Ford I have this '34 coupé. I bought it already built. It's a show-winning car and cost a pile of cash. I used to have one myself back in the 1950s, which we dragged out of a field and got going. I used to race that thing, drag-racing mainly. It was pretty basic. This one's got all the comforts and trim. It's got a nice roof chop on it, a dry-lakes chop. It's my winter hot-rod now, I drive it at least once a week, and the '27 roadster gets a little cold at my age in the winter, so I lay that one up until it gets warm.'

Mike Parti's workshop is in his garage and is full of tools neatly arranged on wall brackets. It all look busy but not chaotic, as

Mike is considered to be a master mechanic, restoring classic motorcycles for clients such as Jay Leno. The shelves all around are laden with engine parts, carburettor set-ups and all manner of things that would make any old-school rat-rodder's mouth water; moreover, it would not escape their notice that Mike Parti still seems to be getting his kicks at well past the age of 66!

OPPOSITE & ABOVE: Mike pictured in his 1927 Ford roadster on different occasions.

ABOVE RIGHT: Taken from Mike Parti's photo album, the picture shows a drag race in the 1950s.

RIGHT: Mike, as a young man in the 1950s, with his original 1934 coupé that he altered every year.

DUSTIN DARROUGH

Dustin Darrough carves wooden tikis and is based in Southern California. Operating under the name of the Von Tiki Trading Company, he was one of a number of traders at the annual Primer Nationals hot-rod gathering in Ventura, California.

The art and culture of the tiki is enjoying a revival at the beginning of the 21st century, thanks in part to the growth of interest in old- school retro and kustom kulture in general, that is so popular in the hot-rod world. *Tiki* is the Maori word for a god, used to describe an image carved in wood or greenstone and used as a talisman against evil spirits. Nowadays, however, the word is applied to all things relating to Polynesian culture, from aloha shirts, exotic fruit cocktails, carved mugs and grass-skirted hula girls. To understand why this sub-culture is popular with the hot-rod fraternity, it is necessary to look back to the California of the late 1930s and '40s.

Don Beach, also known as Don the Beachcomber, opened up a restaurant and bar with a Polynesian theme in Hollywood in 1934, where customers could enjoy Polynesian-type food and cocktails in an environment that resembled a tropical paradise.

The Second World War brought thousands of servicemen into the Pacific theatre of war with Japan. It also exposed young men to an exotic culture that would otherwise have remained a mystery to them. Memories of dusky, grass-skirted maidens, with garlands of flowers around their necks, fuelled the fantasies of many a GI and they

returned home bearing souvenirs of South-Sea islands, including tiki carvings. When hostilities ended, an entrepreneur called Victor Bergeron, or Trader Vic, established a chain of bars with a tropical theme across California, thus beginning the trend that

would ultimately sweep America. It is likely that the idea flourished as a way of banishing the post-war blues and was a reflection of the growing optimism that carried America into the 1950s and '60s. In the movie, *Blue Hawaii*, of 1961, Elvis

Presley further popularized the idea of a perfect paradise.

The tiki craze also influenced the design of home accessories, interior decoration and architecture, and tiki bars were to be found in every town and city across the country

until the fashion began to fade during the 1970s.

Tiki art is now undergoing something of a revival, due to the new nostalgia for hot rods and rockabilly, and interest in the past has never been stronger.

Dustin Darrough, a carver of tikis, describes how the tiki became entwined with the hot-rod scene and kustom kulture in general. Although the fashion for all things Polynesian began to decline in the 1970s, interest in the tiki never quite disappeared. It survived in the surfing community in California, largely because Hawaii is the ultimate surfer's paradise, and artists such as Big Daddy Roth used tiki designs in his t- shirts, keeping the trend alive as part of hot- rod cculture. Now that tattooing has become more acceptable than ever before, there is a demand for tiki-style tattoos.

Dustin's interest in the phenomenon began in the 1980s, when he began to collect artefacts from flea markets and dime stores, left over from the period. It wasn't until 2002, however, that Dustin became actively involved in what he describes as a 'tiki renaissance' and began to carve palm logs into tiki gods. Where they originated, methods of carving tikis vary from one island group to another, from Hawaii, the Cook Islands, Easter Island and New Zealand. In the culture of the South Seas, tikis are made to represent gods of war, fishing, agriculture etc, but Dustin's carvings bear no resemblance to these. He refers to his carvings as good luck charms for the back yard. He believes in a force or

karma that influences how each individual carving turns out, and no two are the same. He also believes that if a tiki is stolen, its karma goes along with it, as well as the luck it brings.

He only uses traditional palm logs and carves them using a chainsaw, chisels, angle-grinders and gougers, while the finish is achieved by burning the carved surfaces with a blowtorch. This burning can be regarded as a ritual by which negative elements are removed, while at the same time giving a pleasing antique look to the carving.

Dustin does not think the tiki will enjoy anything like its popularity it did in the 1950s and '60s, but it will continue to develop a healthy following among the young hot-rodders and rockabilly fans, still nostalgic for an era that has passed.

OPPOSITE: Tiki-carver, Dustin Darrough, plies his trade at the Primer Nationals, in Ventura, California.

LEFT: Tikis carved out of palm logs are popular with the hot-rod set.

TROY TREPANIER

Troy Trepanier, who plies his trade under the description, Rad Rides by Troy, in Manteno, Illinois, is one of the shining lights of the world of professional hot-rodding. Troy is capable of making it onto anyone's top-ten list, as he is one of the most talented and innovative independent car designers in the business, rivalled only by his contemporary, Chip Foose, with whom he often collaborates.

Fast cars must have imprinted themselves in Troy's DNA: he was born in the shade of the Indianapolis Speedway, in the same hospital that unfortunate lndy race drivers would sometimes find themselves after an argument with the Armco barrier. Moreover, both Troy's father and grandfather were similarly mechanically inclined. Troy attributes his talent for metaworking to his grandfather, in whose workshop he liked to hang out, while his father taught him mechanics. His legendary attention to detail a he owes to his grandfather, whose mantra, often-repeated, was that there was only one way to do things; the right way.

Troy acquired his first car courtesy of his grandfather, a 1966 Chevrolet Chevelle, which his grandfather had owned from new. When it broke down, it was given to Troy, then aged 16, who rebuilt it and used it to drive himself to school.

Troy's interest in hot rods and custom cars was awakened following a visit to the Du Quoin Street Machine Nationals, when his eyes were opened to new possibilities. Troy returned home and immediately began

to rebuild the Chevelle, which he painted a vivid raspberry red. The car made it into *Hot Rod* magazine in late 1986, when Troy was still a teenager, which was quite an accomplishment for one so young.

The next car to draw attention to Troy's emerging talent, was project ProBox, a 1960 Chevy Bel Air two-door saloon. He tubbed the rear-wheel wells and fitted 33-inch (84-cm) Mickey Thompson Sportsman tyres, painting the car a lurid turquoise green. This too made it into the pages of

BELOW & OPPOSITE: Troy Trepanier built the roadster, QuadraDeuce, for the Summit Racing company.

LEFT: QuadraDeuce's interior is clean, simple and uncluttered.

OPPOSITE: QuadraDeuce is possibly the most hi-tech 1932 roadster in the world.

Hot Rod magazine, where it was hailed Car of the Year. Troy demonstrated to the world that his car was well-built and reliable by driving it cross-country, something he does with all his personal cars to this day.

Two years later, in 1992, a Troy Trepanier car again featured in *Hot Rod* magazine as Car of the Year. This time it was a 1950 Buick sedanette: on the outside it wore a peach-and-orange paint job and Mickey Thompson Sportsman billet wheels in tubbed rear-wheel wells. But that was not the whole story: under the skin was a completely new Trepanier-built tube chassis, housing a 510-ci (8357-cc) Chevy motor, and boasting electronic fuel injection by John Meaney.

Troy built a number of personal cars over the next few years, all of which earned him magazine features and awards, until Dan Jacobs gave him his first professional build – a 1939 Chevy coupé, called Predator, which won the Goodguys Street Rod of the Year in 1995. His company, Rad Rides by Troy, was born around this time and in ten years has grown from a staff of two to the present-day 13, four of which bear the Trepanier name; it is a family-run business, not large in size, but hugely influential and respected in the business.

The car pictured here is called the

QuadraDeuce, and was built by Troy for Summit Racing. Quite simply, it is the most radical and h-itech 1932 roadster in the world today. The QuadraDeuce transmits 594hp to the asphalt through a custom-built four-wheel-drive assembly, and sports many one-off features, including hand-made parts and extra Trepanier touches.

The all-wheel-drive assembly was built by Troy and Summit Racing, while the front differential and transfer box from a GMC Cyclone was used, together with custom half-shafts made by Summit. The rear is a Corvette ZR-1 differential, while the front suspension is in the style of an Indy car, with fully-adjustable shocks. The wheels are one-off billet specials, running BF Goodrich scorcher tyres, while the big four-piston Baer disc brakes ensure that all those horses can be controlled safely. The exhaust system is configured so that they are invisible and do not hang beneath the car, which is one of Troy's pet hates.

The Deuce body is a Harwood combination of fibreglass and carbon fibre. The hood is steel and the side- panels are made from hand-crafted aluminium. The body is painted in two-tone wild-cherry red, over a smoked-grey, separated by flame graphics. The motor is a small-block Chevy 406ci (6653cc), built by John Lingenfelter.

The interior of the car is as beautifully finished as the outside. Leather bench seats are a traditional touch, among all the hi-tech wizardry, such as the Billet Specialties tilting steering column and steering wheel.

When Henry Ford's 1932 models were rolling off the production line almost 75 years ago, who could have dreamt that the design would be inspiring 21st-century car-builders like Troy Trepanier to create wonderful cars like these.

ABOVE LEFT & RIGHT: Close inspection reveals that the front wheels are also driven, making the QuadraDeuce an all-wheel-drive hot rod.

OPPOSITE: The colour-matched engine shroud is a Troy Trepanier signature touch.

CHAPTER TEN

HOT-ROD EVENTS

ROCK 'N' ROLL AT HEMSBY

Hemsby is a small seaside town on the east coast of England, near the town of Great Yarmouth, and has been the venue for rock 'n' roll weekender events for almost 20 years. Held twice a year, during May and October, the events begin on a Wednesday and finish on a Monday night and are aimed at aficionados of 1950s rockabilly music. The event is famous for presenting as many original artists of the period as possible, many of whom are known only to serious students of the 1950s music scene. Contemporary rock 'n' roll bands from all over the world also take part, and music is played 24 hours a day, allowing eventers literally to rock around the clock. Not only has the sub-culture been flourishing in the last two decades in the UK, it has also been similarly strong in France and Sweden during this time, in fact, long before nostalgic feelings for the 1950s resurfaced in the USA.

The Hemsby 'rockin' crowd', as they call themselves, are extremely knowledgeable on all aspects of their favourite era, and great emphasis is put on wearing exactly the 'right' clothes. Original period pieces are preferred over reproductions, and many vendors specializing in antique clothing can be found

in and around the confines of the event. Furniture and ornaments, and indeed any objects connected with the 1950s are highly collectible, as is original vinyl dating from the period.

A high proportion of the Hemsby eventers understandably favour the transport of the 1950s and '60s, and this ranges from British cars, such as the Vauxhall Cresta, to all types of classic American cars; these can be seen cruising around Hemsby throughout the day and night. Hemsby is centred around a Pontin's holiday camp: this and other such camps powerfully evoke the 1950s, while the small town has its share of gaudy neon-lit amusement arcades and fish-and-chip shops.

In recent years, there has been a noticeable increase in the incidence of hot rods at the event, many of which fall into the rat-rod category. The numbers of old-school chopped and bobbed motorcycles, both British and American, have also increased tremendously, so much so that Hemsby is becoming as well known as a hot-rod and chop meeting place as it is a festival of 1950s rock 'n' roll.

RIGHT and OPPOSITE: As long as the sun shines, live rockabilly music and dancing on the beach are popular features of the Hemsby events.

on the hallowed lawns of the Pebble Beach Concours d'Élegance for the first time, normally the province of the seriously rich, and more usually accustomed to Duesenbergs, V16 Cadillacs and Delages. In earlier times, the idea that well-heeled classic car owners should rub shoulders with hot-rod outlaws, representing opposite ends of the automotive spectrum, would have seemed preposterous – indeed, many hot-rodders and classic car owners still hold this negative view. Certainly the editorial staff of *Rodder's Journal* was still unsure that the twain should meet, so it ran the Pebble Beach story and counterbalanced it with pictures of young outlaw rodders, tearing along the Hemsby sands, thus recognizing the history of the hot-rod scene.

A selection of the photographs published here first appeared in the *Rodder's Journal*, a high-quality quarterly publication, much revered in the hot-rod world. The year in question was 1998 (*Rodder's Journal* No 8), and the Hemsby feature, spread over ten pages, was designed to capture the spirit of the old-school hot-rodders of 1940/'50s California. Flat black or primer Model As, Ts and Deuces, many sporting wire wheels and powered by flathead V8s, were shown being run along the beach, sending up plumes of sand into the air, while members of the Deuces, Concordes and A-Bomber car clubs, wearing painted flying jackets, rolled-up Levis and engineer boots, looked on while drinking beer.

That same year, hot rods were allowed

OPPOSITE: A roadster basks in the sun, while receiving admiring glances from the onlookers, as they enjoy their beer.

LEFT: Hot rods and classic cars line up on the beach.

OPPOSITE: A Chevy Impala provides the right backdrop to a party on the beach.

ABOVE LEFT: This beautiful Mercury has come all the way from France for a rock 'n' roll weekend.

ABOVE: The Hemsby girls put a great deal of effort into getting their hair and dresses right for the evening's dancing.

FAR LEFT: Many booths in and around the event sell antique 1950s clothes and paraphernalia.

LEFT: A member of the Deuces car club gets the 'look' just right.

OPPOSITE: The strip of amusement arcades and burger stalls provide a colourful background to this Ford coupé.

LEFT: Members of the Deuces car club take a break from tearing up the beach.

PAGE 322: Hundreds of spectators gather on the sand dunes to admire the rods and classic cars below.

PAGE 323: Leather flying jackets, rolled up Levis, and engineer boots are de rigueur for the hot- rod look.

ABOVE: 1927 Ford roadsters in primer and matt-black paint evoke the dry-lakes scene of the late 1940s.

ABOVE RIGHT: An historic Deuce roadster.

RIGHT: Two Swedish hot-rodders from the A-Bombers car club, put their 1927 roadster through its paces.

OPPOSITE: Looking cool in the hot sunshine, these hot-rodders in their early 20s are typical of the new blood that is now entering the scene.

PAGE 326: Searching for that collector's vinyl or original 1950s clothes is an obsession for many at Hemsby.

PAGE 327: Four people can be fitted into a hiboy roadster, as long as they are all good friends.

OPPOSITE: Streams of hot rods cruise the streets of Hemsby throughout the day and night.

ABOVE LEFT: Flat primer paint with pinstriping on the hood is a popular look with the young set.

ABOVE: The Deuces check their rear suspension for damage.

LEFT: Power-sliding a turtle-decked roadster is what it's all about.

PRIMER NATIONALS – RAT RODS & ROCK & ROLL

The Primer Nationals were established in 2003, when Dave Hansen and John Parker decided there was a demand for a 'Kustom Kulture' feature to celebrate old-style hot-rodding and chopping motorcycles. The show attracts the home-built variety of custom car and bike, and billet barges, over-chromed money pits and trailer queens are not welcome.

The 2005 event, photographed here, was only the third such meeting, but since the first, attendance has doubled from around 300 to over 600 show cars. Over 150 vendors also turned up to peddle their wares, and all aspects of Kuston Kulture was represented: this included tiki artists, pinstripers, automotive artists, and there were all manner of custom accessories and 1950s memorabilia, all shown against a background of live bands playing rock 'n' roll and rockabilly music. Most of those who attended the show seemed to be under 40, which reflects the new wave of interest in all things old-school.

This movement, which seems to have been driven by the Japanese interest in

ABOVE: This flat-black five-window coupé has had a severe top chop.

OPPOSITE: Pinstripers are constantly busy.

nostalgia, has spread out and become popular all over the USA, UK, France, and especially Scandanavia, though old-style hod-rodding never really ever went away in Sweden. It would appear to be a reaction against the high-dollar, billet-laden vehicles that gained popularity in the 1990s, when success in custom shows was suddenly beyond the reach of persons of more modest means; this

effectively excluded most young people from the scene. Thankfully, there were those who still remembered what hot-rodding had been all about, back in the old days, when people worked on their cars themselves, making use of what was available and spending very little as a result. Parallels can be seen in the music scene, when rock stars began to be perceived as 'dinosaurs' in the mid to late 1970s and a

scene developed among the young called punk rock. It was a back-to-basics movement, that returned to the roots of rock music, to a time when passion and enthusiasm were more important than technical perfection.

And so it happened in the hot-rod world, when a punk-type movement, that rejected the consumerism and excess of the 1990s, returned to the simpler, more basic roots of

hot-rodding as it had existed in the 1940s and '50s. This nostalgic movement can collectively be referred to as 'Greasy Kulture', a term coined by a Brit, who established an e-zine of the same name in around 2000. At that time, there was precious little in the mainstream press that covered the burgeoning scene, but in 2005 many underground publications, websites and mainstream magazines, such as *Ol' Skool Rodz*, now exist.

As with all sub-cultures, this movement is not confined to cars and bikes – the music and clothes of the 1940s and '50s are also important elements.

At the Primer Nationals, held in the beachside town of Ventura, Southern California, rockabilly provides the backing-track to the day's events. The guys usually wear their hair in rock 'n' roll DA style, with long sideburns, and often sport goatee beards. The girls favour the hairstyles of the 1940s – hair dyed copper-red or jet-black, fringed in a Betty Boop style. They also dress in either 1940s or '50s style.

Ventura provides a suitable backdrop for this event, in that it has the slightly seedy, dated feel typical of American and British seaside resorts. The 1950s-style crumbly motels and the bowling alley, which is the focus of the evening's activities, are places where a rusty primer or flat pickup look perfectly at home.

Dave Hanson and John Parker have created a wonderful event, which will be held on Labor day from now on. Hopefully, it will retain its friendly club atmosphere and not grow too large, becoming a victim of its own success.

LEFT: Rockabilly girls in party mood at the Primer Nationals.

ABOVE :A severely-chopped sedan sits outside the bowling alley in Ventura, California.

OPPOSITE: Old-school choppers go hand-in-hand with old-school rods.

PAGE 334: A slammed-to-the-ground Model T rat rod.

PAGE 335: A Ford pickup rat rod.

OPPOSITE: This 1927 Ford roadster sports slash-cut carb stacks and zoomie headers.

LEFT: This couple are typical of the young blood coming into the hot-rod scene.

PAGE 338: Offenhauser cylinder-heads are an authentic tuning accessory.

PAGE 339: This Model T roadster has a nicely pinstriped and louvred turtle deck.

RIGHT & OPPOSITE: This five-window coupé is distinguished by the triple down-draught carbs and Offenhauser cylinder-heads.

PAGE 342: More young couples enjoying the Primer Nationals in 2005.

PAGE 343: This young owner is justly proud of his flat-black roadster.

ABOVE LEFT: A cool 1933 Dodge coupé lurks in the shadows.

ABOVE: This pickup is a good example of the 'outlaw' style, made popular by Jimmy Shine.

LEFT & OPPOSITE: This Model T has a colourful Indian blanket interior, which was very common in the 1940s and '50s.

PAGE 346: The drop-axle and leaf-spring arrangement ensures this roadster sits low to the ground.

PAGE 347: A flathead V8-powered Hiboy.

OPPOSITE: This rat-rod pickup is hiding an hydraulic suspension system which controls the ride height.

LEFT: A flathead V8-powered 1934 Ford three-window coupé.

BELOW LEFT: A nice example of a 1934 coupé.

BELOW: This Model T looks strange, sitting on modern radial tyres.

PAGE 350: This five-window coupé belongs to a member of the Immortals car club, California.

PAGE 351: This Ford retains a functional wooden pickup bed.

HOT AUGUST NIGHTS

'The Biggest Little City in The World', is the legend emblazoned on the archway that straddles the Main Street at Reno, Nevada. Certainly it is a little city, but for ten days in August each year it becomes the venue for one of the biggest gatherings of 1950s and '60s American automobiles in the world. Five thousand cars are officially registered in the rally and from 5–10,000 classic cars and hot rods are also in attendance during the course of the event.

Over 170,000 people are attracted to the Reno/Sparks twin-city area, which is situated in the northern Nevada desert, just across the border from California. Reno and Sparks are gambling towns first and foremost – almost mini versions of Las Vegas. The towns are dominated by casinos – some of them of gigantic proportions.

The 'Hot August Nights' car show is the most important revenue-generating event, not only for the city of Reno itself, but also for the casinos and hotels that cater to visitors. It is a gathering of custom metal so large, that it is probably visible from space!

During the ten days of the event, there are countless Show and Shines on offer, together with auctions, huge swap meets, free concerts, featuring stars of the 1960s and '70s, and nightly cruises, while celebrities

RIGHT: A classic Ford on custom wheels.

OPPOSITE: Cruising under the famous Reno arch.

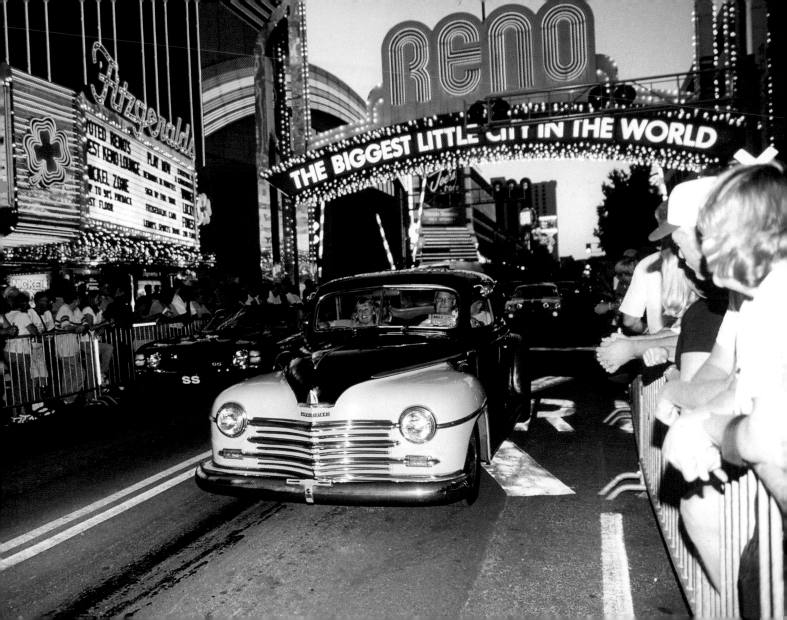

such as the cast of *American Graffiti* make themselves available to fans for photos and autographs.

Huge casinos, such as the Peppermill, Reno Hilton and the Atlantis, hold daily car shows with probably 1,000 cars on show each time, while Hot August Nights provides a visual overload, as acres of chrome and glitzy paint jobs compete with each other beneath the relentless desert sun.

The best part of the whole event is the nightly cruise through the neon-drenched streets of Reno, when columns of 1950s, '60s and early '70s cars stream through the famous archway, periodically interrupted by huge Santa Fe trains, which actually pass through the centre of the city. This gives the place an uncanny feeling of the Wild West and the plaintive sound of the train's whistles and bells are strangely evocative of Western movies.

The people who bring their cars to show at Reno can be classified as belonging to the 'baby boomer' generation, born after the

OPPOSITE: A Ford Tudor sedan patrols downtown Reno.

ABOVE: A nice example of an old-school flat-black roadster.

Second World War, many of whom are either reliving their youth, or the youth they would have preferred, had they had the money or opportunity at the time. Married couples predominate, whose children have long flown the nest; consequently, the event is quite a laid-back affair, with none of the high jinks and smoking tyres that characterizes rat-rod events. It is immediately noticeable that the new wave of primer rat-rod cars are not represented at Hot August Nights, apart from a very few examples, and it is probably true to say that the majority of hot-rod and custom-car owners did not build their own vehicles, but bought turn-key cars from a hot-rod shop: nevertheless this keeps a lot of people in work in both the custom and classic-car industries.

OPPOSITE: Cruising in an early 1940s Ford street rod.

RIGHT: This is the standard of detailing required to attract the judges' attention at the Show and Shines.

PAGE 358: Its owner must have paid top dollar for this luxury street rod.

PAGE 359: This 1948 Oldsmobile sits a lot closer to the asphalt than the original designer intended.

ABOVE LEFT: Ford sedans make luxurious street rods.

ABOVE: Classics on show on the streets of Sparks, Reno's twin town.

LEFT: This classic early-1950s Chevrolet has a period air-conditioning unit on the passenger window.

OPPOSITE: A 1934 sedan with chopped roof.

RIGHT: Rods, customs and classics – they all cruise the casino-lined streets of Reno.

OPPOSITE: Hank's 1940 Ford glints in the hot sunshine outside The Nugget casino.

PAGES 364 & 365: This hi-tech 1933 coupé is at the far end of the spectrum, as far as old-school is concerned.

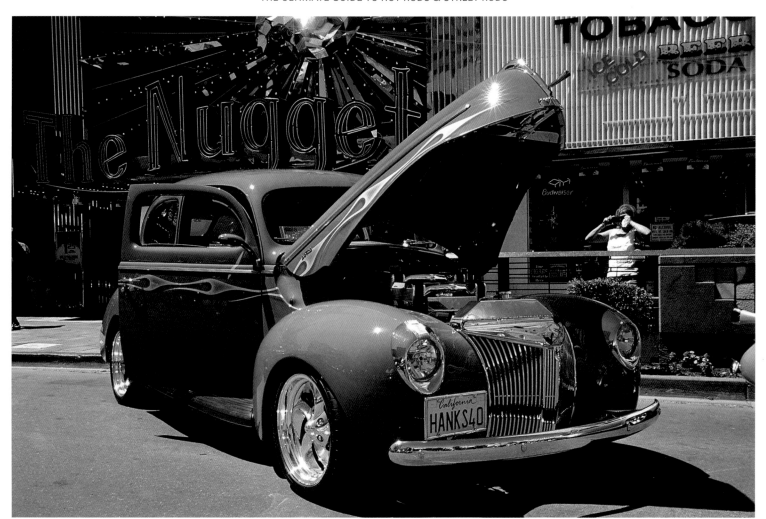

OPPOSITE: A 1955 Chevy Bel Air with flames.

ABOVE LEFT: Woodies are a popular sub-genre in the world of classics and customs.

ABOVE: An Oldsmobile coupé in a Reno Show and Shine.

LEFT: The decoration is typical of 1990s style.

PAGE 368: Not all Ford five-window coupés have roof chops.

PAGE 369: The Hot August Nights cruise attracts thousands of spectators, who applaud each car as it passes.

LEFT Some people prefer to turn luxury limos into street rods.

BELOW LEFT: Cruising in style in a flame-decorated cabriolet.

BELOW: Henry Ford could never have envisaged the way people would individualize his production cars.

OPPOSITE: The Reno Hilton, and many of the other casino-hotel complexes, host huge car shows every day.

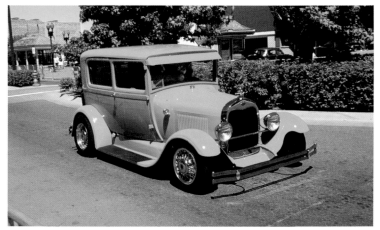

OPPOSITE & LEFT: This three-window Deuce coupé is very well detailed in the engine department.

PAGE 374: This panel-truck/woody/surf-wagon has a lot going on.

PAGE 375: An impressive array of Ford coupés line the streets of Reno.

LEFT: Burning up the strip in a 1950s classic.

BELOW LEFT: Hot-rodding 1970s-style.

BELOW: Hot flames and the Mercury is rising.

OPPOSITE: A not so sedate sedan!

PAGE 378: A fully-fendered 1934 roadster.

PAGE 379: A Chevy-powered hot Deuce roadster.

RIGHT: Originally there would have been a flathead V8 under the hood.

OPPOSITE: This 1934 coupé was shown at the Peppermill casino Show 'n Shine.

PAGES 382 & 383: This fully-fendered roadster looks set for drag-strip action, if the wheelie bars are anything to go by.

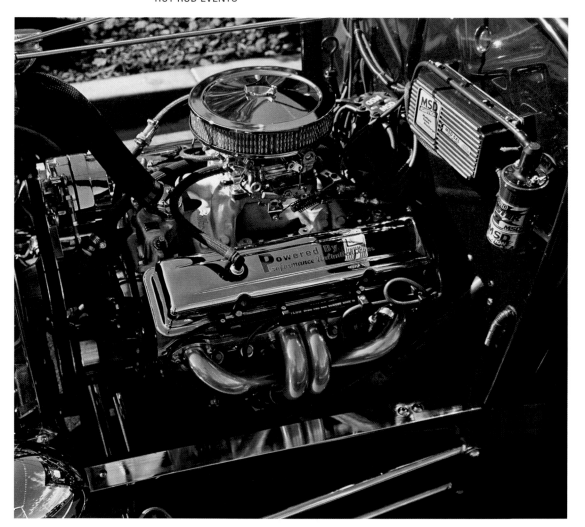

OPPOSITE: A very nice Pete and Jake-influenced 1934 three-window coupé.

ABOVE LEFT: Much painstaking work has gone into fabricating this car's bodywork.

ABOVE: Spectators are invited to sit in this roadster and be photographed.

LEFT: James Dean actually drove this Mercury.

OPPOSITE & LEFT: A jazzy paint scheme does much to lift this Chevy-powered Tudor sedan.

GOODGUYS SHOW, DALLAS

The Goodguys Rod and Custom Association was founded by Gary Meadors, its president, in 1983, and is the leading US promoter and stager of custom car shows. Goodguys is a brotherhood of hot-rod enthusiasts numbering over 70,000 members from all over the globe. Goodguys organizes 22 events all over the USA, some of which are two-day affairs attracting over 25,000 visitors, while others are larger four-day blockbusters, which can attract more than 100,000 visitors.

Rod & Custom events, such as the gathering in Dallas, Texas, photographed here, are a feast for the eyes of any auto enthusiast. Acres and acres of the best the hot-rod world has to offer is on show. The public is able to see at close quarters the incredibly high standard of finish achieved in these examples of automotive art. Hoods are usually raised to display amazing arrays of polished and chromed motor components, such as carbs, turbos and superchargers, and not a hint of oil or grease is to be found in any of the engine bays. Owners even clean and polish the insides of the exhaust outlets,

RIGHT: Goodguys shows are real family events, as this cowboy clown would suggest.

OPPOSITE: The cars line up in front of the Southfork Ranch, immortalized in the TV series, Dallas.

thus eliminating any soot that might sully a judge's fingertip test.

The family atmosphere is a feature of a Goodguys event, where entire families sit beside their pride and joy, picnicking from barbecues and enjoying the sun. They are always ready to answer questions from a curious public, and people are able to get up close and and personal and peer into the cars, admiring the interiors which are every bit as finished and interesting as the outsides. A cardinal rule which must be observed at all times, however, is LOOK BUT DO NOT TOUCH!

The displays accompanying some of the cars are often quite ingenious and amusing. One can be sure that a roadrunner and coyote will feature somewhere or other, while others lay out period picnic sets, complete with plastic burgers. One exhibitor's attention to period detail went to the length of leaving a Hershey chocolate bar-wrapper from the 1950s lying carelessly on the dash!

The Goodguys also put on shows aimed at the Street Machine crowd, which tends to be younger, and which appreciates hi-tech pickup trucks or late-1960s muscle cars.

The event pictured here was held in the grounds of the Southfork Ranch, near Dallas, famous as the home of J R Ewing and his family in the TV series, Dallas. Visitors were able to leave the show and wander through the house, where they would recognize the things they had already seen on TV.

The Goodguys also stages vintage drag races, where fans can experience the nostalgic race cars of the 1960s and watch gassers blasting up the quarter-mile. The prime event is held each spring at the historic Famoso Raceway in Bakersfield, California.

A great family day out is guaranteed at any Goodguys event, and knowledgeable experts are as welcome to the hot-rod scene as keen newcomers.

OPPOSITE: An outstanding example of a Mercury street rod.

LEFT: Coyote often turns up at Goodguys shows.

PAGE 392: The clean lines of this Ford custom are enhanced by the elimination of door handles.

PAGE 393: This flame-decorated roadster deserves all the admiration it gets.

OPPOSITE: A classy line-up of custom Fords.

ABOVE: Roadrunner and coyote themes occur again and again.

LEFT: A huge blown Chevy motor spells big horsepower.

PAGE 396: This cabriolet has the scalloped paint job popular in the 1990s.

PAGE 397: Goodguys puts on displays like this all across the USA.

RIGHT: The sun highlights the metallic painted flames on this 1940 Ford.

OPPOSITE: This 1939 Ford has been finished in pearlescent paint.

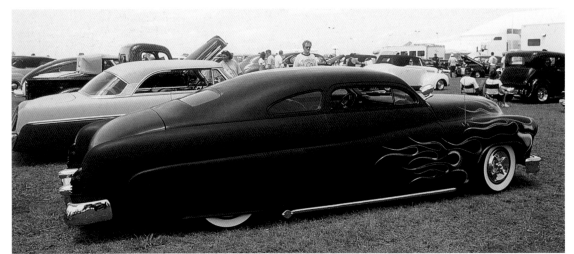

LEFT: A slammed-to-the-ground Mercury custom.

BELOW LEFT: A Model T pickup on billet wheels.

BELOW: A Chevrolet station wagon with its toy replica.

OPPOSITE: A colourful line-up of Ford commercials.

PACIFIC COAST DREAM MACHINE SHOW

The Pacific Coast Dream Machine Show takes place on the last Sunday in April each year. It is held at Half-Moon Bay airport, just south of San Francisco on Pacific Coast Highway One. For an event that only lasts a day, this is a truly remarkable gathering. American automobiles are the main attraction, and over 2,000 cars from the 20th and 21st centuries are on show. This being California, the birthplace of hot-rodding, it is no surprise to see that the majority of entries are fantastic examples of hot rods, street rods, street machines and custom cars, rubbing shoulders with the restored classics that provided the raw material for the rodder's art.

Cars converge on this oceanside airport, long before the sun's rays appear over the hills that lie to the east. The early riser is rewarded by a roadside extravaganza of the American automobile in all its forms, as a rolling calvacade of motoring history passes along Highway One.

The best place to see and photograph the hot rods and custom cars is on the airport perimeter road, as the cars pass on their way to the display area, which is always crowded with cars and people, making it difficult to get a good look at the lines of a car. As they arrive, one is able to appreciate the sound of

RIGHT: There are plenty of original classics at Half-Moon Bay: this Model A demonstrates that not everything was chopped in California.

OPPOSITE: A 1940s Ford street rod glides past.

engines being revved up for the benefit of the onlookers, and a little smoking rubber is created if the marshals are not looking.

One needs to attend this show if one never realized a farm tractor could be a hot rod too. The main entertainment is provided by the tractor-pulling contest, in which a tractor or truck pulls a weighted sled along a loose dirt course in an attempt to drag it to the finish line. Success is measured by how far the sled is pulled or how quickly the course is completed. As with many motorsports, this has become highly competitive and classes have been extended to include nitrous-burning tractors, some with multiple Chevy V8 mills. These super-hot tractors bear only a superficial resemblance to their farming cousins, though a John Deere will at least be green-and-yellow and a Massey-Ferguson red.

Half-Moon Bay also hosts an incredible display of aircraft, including the favourite Second World War Warbirds, which do fly-bys from time to time.

Alongside the classic cars, rods, muscle cars and modern sports cars, the spectators are treated to displays of all types of race-car machinery. Top fuel dragsters and funny cars, gassers, and even ones that are jet-powered, fire up their engines to give the onlookers an awesome sense of horsepower. As show organizer Bob Senz points out: 'This is a show for everyman, open to anyone who wants to turn up, pay that fee and line up.' There is no elitism here, and one will see a million-dollar Packard or Duesenberg standing next to a rusty but equally cherished Dodge Charger.

OPPOSITE: If it moves, give it some flames!

LEFT: This Chevy has had a mild custom job, and has retained the original trim.

PAGE 406: 1957 Chevys are always popular.

PAGE 407: Some opt for the comfort of a luxury street-rod coupé.

LEFT: A Chevy Del Ray two-door, sitting on custom wheels.

BELOW LEFT: There are some over-embellished vehicles on show.

BELOW: A classic T Ford bucket.

OPPOSITE: This Oldsmobile has been transformed from family car to race car.

PAGE 410: A rare hot-rodded Caddy coupé.

PAGE 411: A nice example of a shaved and lowered Oldsmobile.

RIGHT: Where did this craze for weeping child mannekins come from, and why?

OPPOSITE: Here, the smooth curves of the 1940s are contrasted with the angular lines of the 1930s.

LEFT: Even the family station wagon cannot escape the custom treatment.

BELOW LEFT: A chopped and channelled Oldsmobile.

BELOW: A Ford phaeton-bodied roadster rolls into Half-Moon Bay airport.

OPPOSITE: Paint and custom wheels are enough to give this classic a street-rod look.

PAGES 416 & 417: Many owners keep their cars in standard form, apart from giving them hot motors under the hood and custom wheels.

NSRA ANNUAL HOT-ROD DRAGS

The National Street Rod Association was established in the UK in 1972, when a group of drag racers and street-rod builders got together for a beer in a public house. In one year, membership had grown to 250, one of whom was Keith Moon, legendary wild-man drummer of The Who rock band. Their first 'run' was held in 1973 at the holiday camp site of Billing Aquadrome, and was christened the Summer Fun Run, when, by all accounts, five real rods (T buckets) turned up along with 35 'others'.

By 1975 the membership had doubled to over 500 and the NSRA was given its own enclosure at Santa Pod, one of the premier venues for drag racing in the UK.

The annual Hot-Rod Drags, photographed here in 2005, were held at the Shakespeare County Raceway, a well-established dragstrip near historic Stratford-upon-Avon. The event attracts hot-rodders from all corners of the UK, and a glance around the many hundreds of cars in attendance makes it immediately obvious that the hot-rod scene in the British Isles is in very good health indeed.

The most striking feature of this event

ABOVE: This rat-rod roadster looks like a jalopy racer.

OPPOSITE: An alcohol-fuelled dragster Deuce.

was the number of primer rat rods in attendance. This old-school hot-rod movement is having a big effect upon the scene all over the world and is especially popular with the younger crowd, many of whom are also involved in the rockabilly scene. The interest that has been generated in the younger rodders bodes well for the future of hot-rodding, not only in the UK, but also in the USA. In fact, the hot-rod scene has probably never been stronger.

The big attraction of this event, apart from the nostalgic rails and gassers of the 1960s, is the fact that everyone can race their rods up the quarter-mile or 'run what you brung', and all that is necessary is a valid driving licence, a small fee, and success in a scrutiny test to see if the vehicle is safe.

Watching T buckets, Deuces, coupés, outlaw Anglias, gassers, and even little kids in their lawn mower-engined mini rods race up the strip keeps hundreds of fans enthralled for the whole weekend.

This is an event with a real 'buzz' to it.

In the main, the rodders dress in classic 1950s style, with greased-back hair, white t-shirts, rolled-up Levis, and engineer boots – and that's not only the guys! Huge camping facilities, rock 'n' roll music, and an on-site late bar enables rodders to park up, put away their car keys and party until dawn.

Next morning sees many a bleary-eyed greaser, supping hot, steaming tea, while lining their queasy stomachs with a traditional English breakfast of bacon, sausages, eggs and beans, before firing up the flathead, and getting in line for a head-clearing blast up the strip – a perfect hangover cure, if ever there was one.

Car shows are great, cruises are great, but run-what-you-brung weekenders at a drag strip, smoking rubber, and having a wonderful time, are greater still!

OPPOSITE: 'Run what you brung' is the motto of the annual Hot-Rod Drags.

LEFT: A primered Model T roadster cruises the camp site.

BELOW LEFT: A nice example of a 1932 highboy, with Duvall windshield and cowgirl.

BELOW: The outlaw Anglias are a favourite with the drag-race fans.

PAGE 422: This roadster has a 'track'-style front end.

PAGE 423: This flathead five-window coupé is an extreme example of the rat-rod style.

OPPOSITE & LEFT: Members of the Rocketeers car club await their turn in the fire lane at the Shakespeare County raceway.

ABOVE: The kids get to run their lawn-mower-engined mini rods at the NSRA drags.

PAGE 426: Rudimentary straps keep the hood in place, while the windshield has been removed to reduce drag.

PAGE 427: A well-turned-out flathead-powered roadster is driven by a rather young pilot.

LEFT: A nice lakester-style Ford roadster.

BELOW LEFT: This nostalgic drag racer has a narrowed coupé body.

BELOW: This Deuce highboy roadster looks quick, with its swept-back Duvall windshield.

OPPOSITE: A three-window Deuce coupé lines up for drag-race action.

OPPOSITE: Note that all the hot-rodders waiting to drag-race their cars seem to be in the 20–30 age group and most are wearing 1950s-style clothes.

LEFT & BELOW LEFT: A change of carburettor got this 1932 roadster shooting rooster tails of dirt.

BELOW: A 1957 Chevrolet pickup truck.

CHAPTER ELEVEN

HOT RODS AT THE PETERSEN MUSEUM

Robert E 'Pete' Petersen has been a key figure in the world of hot rods since 1947. He was initially engaged by Southern California Timing Association (SCTA) to help run a public-relations exercise to improve the image of the hot-rod movement by organizing and regulating it under the SCTA, and by adding respectability to what had hitherto been perceived as disreputable. It was at this time that he also helped establish *Hot Rod* magazine, the first publication of the future Petersen publishing empire.

The success of Petersen Publishing enabled Robert and his wife, Margie, to found the Petersen Automotive Museum, one of the largest in the USA, having received donations amounting to $30 million. In 1994 the Petersen Automotive Museum on Wilshire Boulevard opened its doors onto the famous 'Miracle Mile'. Dedicated to the history of the automobile, the museum consists of 300,000sq ft (27870m²) of floor space, spread over four floors. At any one time, there are over 150 cars, trucks or motorcycles on display.

The first floor houses exhibits that relate the automobile with everyday life, illustrated by lifelike dioramas.

The second is where permanent exhibits

are kept, such as race cars, hot rods and motorcycles, together with celebrity and movie cars. The Hollywood gallery houses exhibitions that are regularly changed – Muscle Cars or Cars of Heads of State, for example.

The third floor, the May Family Children's Discovery Center has many hands-on experiences designed to help children understand scientific and engineering principals as they relate to the automobile, while the fourth has been turned into a glass-covered penthouse conference centre.

The hot rods exhibited include a 1950 Mercury, standing in a period workshop, in the process of being 'lead-sledded'. Another depicts a Ford hot rod undergoing an engine change, using a timber A-frame, while elsewhere there is a typical speed shop with flathead tuning parts and many of the hop-up accessories available at the time.

The centrepiece of the second floor is the permanent exhibition of Bruce Meyer's hot-rod collection. Meyer, an avid collector of historic automobiles, has a particular soft spot for hot rods, and can frequently be seen at hot-rod drive-ins at the controls of one of his cars. He has acquired a number of significant historic hot rods, many of which he has had restored, some by So-Cal, such as the Pierson brothers' coupé and Alex Xydias'

OPPOSITE & RIGHT: This 1923 Model T won the America's Most Beautiful Roadster award twice, in 1971 and 1975. The mural paint scheme is typical of the 1970s.

LEFT: This roadster was built in 1969, its style and paint highly influenced by the work of Ed 'Big Daddy' Roth.

BELOW LEFT: Designed by Chip Foose and built at Boyd Coddington's, this Deuce 0032 roadster won the AMBR award twice, in 1996 and 2000.

BELOW: The Piersen brothers' coupé, now owned by Bruce Meyer, was still racing in the 1990s.

OPPOSITE: The Thacker and Shine roadster, on show in the foyer of the Petersen museum on Wilshire Boulevard, Los Angeles.

belly-tank racer. Other significant cars in the Bruce Meyer collection are the Duane Spencer roadster, Ed Roth's Outlaw, the Niekamp roadster, and Boyd Coddington's Boydster I.

Thanks to Bruce Meyer and the Petersen Museum, the hot-rod enthusiast is able to see many key historic hot rods all in one place and at close quarters – all for a ten-dollar admission fee.

LEFT: Ed Roth's Outlaw was the first of his one-off creations and made its debut in 1959.

OPPOSITE: This 1932 Boydster was designed to be sold as a kit to clients or could be built to order by Boyd Coddington.

PAGE 438: The museum created this display showing a Mercury undergoing the process of being lead-sledded.

PAGE 439: The unmistakable Batmobile was designed and built by the legendary George Barris.

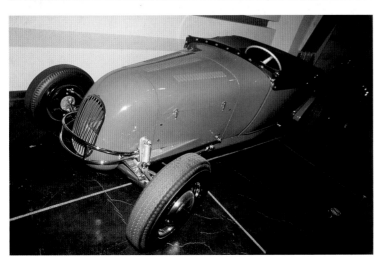

ABOVE LEFT: This 1932 Ford Hiboy roadster is an original 1950s salt-flat racer. It set a record of 142.97mph (230.08km/h) in 1954 at Bonneville.

ABOVE: The Instant T was the first replica made available in kit form to the public in 1962. It was developed by Ted McMullen.

LEFT: The first-ever winner of the AMBR award in 1950, this 1929 Ford was built by Bill Niekamp.

OPPOSITE: This classic Deuce coupé has an Italmeccanica supercharger and Ardun heads.

PAGE 442: Another double AMBR winner at the Oakland Roadster show in 1967 and 1968 is The Invader, built by Don Borth.

PAGE 443
ABOVE LEFT: This 1927 roadster was built by Roy Brizio to go on the 50th-anniversary cover of Hot Rod magazine.

ABOVE RIGHT: Boyd Coddington built this 1933 Ford Victoria, once owned by actor Nicolas Cage.

BELOW LEFT: This 1932 Ford Hiboy roadster was raced by the Berardini brothers in 1950.

BELOW RIGHT:
This 1932 roadster was specially built for Robert E Petersen, the publisher of Hot Rod magazine, and the museum's founder.

1932 FORD
Deuce Coupe

Collection of Bruce Meyer

GLOSSARY

A-pillar The sheetmetal section, located on each side of the windshield between the roof and the main body, that has to be cut when chopping the top.

Alky Alcohol fuel for racing, also known as methyl alcohol or methanol, a very high-octane fuel.

Ardun Heads Created by Zora Arkus-Duntov (circa 1947), the Ardun Manufacturing company fabricated overhead-valve cylinder heads with hemispherical combustion chambers that could be bolted to the Ford V-8 60 (flathead) block. Precursor of the Chrysler Hemi, Ardun heads delivered considerable horsepower gains for hot-rodders and racers privileged enough to be able to afford them.

Belly Pan A custom fabricated underbody piece, used to aid airflow under the car's body – often made of sheet aluminum or steel.

Cal-Neva California-Nevada Timing Association.

Cammer Any engine with an overhead camshaft.

Carson Top Removable hardtops made famous by the Carson Co as early as the 1930s, these tops were a hot trend in the early '50s for custom rodders. George and Sam Barris in Southern California were especially impressed with Carson Tops and applied several to their creations.

Channelled Both a hot rod and custom term pertaining to dropping the car body over the frame to reduce the profile or overall height of the car. The process requires sectioning the firewall, cutting the perimeter of the floor pan, and then welding back to desired height. For early hot rods and dry-lakes cars, this was done to reduce wind resistance and lower the centre of gravity for stability at high speeds. For custom rodders, it was often done for more aesthetic/artistic purposes.

Chopped Similar to channelled, this hot rod and custom term pertains only to the top or roof of the car. By horizontally cutting sections of metal from the a-pillars, door pillars and rear quarter panels, one could lower the roof line, which often resulted in a more sinister appearance.

Cogs Hot-rod term for gears.

Continental Kit A popular bolt-on customization kit for the rear end of 1950s cars. In varying degrees of quality, most kits usually consisted of an external tyre carrier, with stainless steel tyre ring, indented faceplate, drop centre gravel guard, bumper extensions, and a licence light.

Crank Common abbreviation for crankshaft.

D O A term from the early years for an engine equipped with dual overhead camshafts.

Dual Set-Up Early hot-rod term for an engine using a dual intake manifold, equipped with two carburettors.

Fade (Fadeaways) Custom rodder term, where the extruded front fender section gradually flows into the rear extruded fender section, while flowing with the car's body lines.

Fender Skirts Panels covering the rear wheel well, leaving only the bottom part of the rear wheels exposed.

Filled Axle A dropped axle that has both sides of the I-beam section filled with metal at the bend to provide added strength.

Flathead An engine with its valves located in the cylinder block, rather than in the head, the head itself being a plain, flat casting. The term is used particularly to indicate a Ford V-8 engine, built between 1932 and 1955. It could also indicate a Ford four-cylinder Model A, B, or C four-cylinder engine.

Gow Job An obscure pre-Second World War term for a car with a modified engine, apparently derived from gow out (see below). No longer used.

Gow Out Early term meaning to accelerate rapidly. One theory has it that 'gow' is simply a mispronunciation of 'go'. No longer used.

Guide Lights Externally mounted headlights (found on late 1930s cars) that had a small light attached to the top of the headlight housing.

Headers Individual exhaust pipes, usually welded steel tubing, but sometimes cast iron, in various shapes and diameters to reduce exhaust back pressure.

Hides Tyres, eg, to 'boil the hides' – to spin the rear tyres.

Highboy Stock-body roadster with the stock fenders and bumpers removed – usually, but not limited to a 1932 Ford.

Hop-Up, Hot Iron Pre-Second World War terms for a car with a modified engine.

Hot Rod Post-Second World War (after 1945) term for a car with a modified engine.

Jiggler An early hot-rodder's term for a rocker arm.

Jug An early hot-rodder's term for a carburettor.

Juice Brakes Hydraulic brakes as opposed to mechanical brakes. Same as squirt brakes.

Lakester Class designation (after 1950) of cars with custom-made bodywork that was streamlined but had exposed wheels.

Lead Sled Slang for a custom car derived from the use of lead as a filler for smoothing custom body effects.

Lid An early hot-rodder's term for cylinder head.

Locked Rear End An early term for a straight-through drive system with the left and right rear axle shafts fused together at the ring gear. Commonly referred to today as 'posi-traction'.

Mill Any engine.

Modified A dry-lakes class designation for a car which didn't fit in the roadster class, usually with a single-seat sprint-car-type body but cut off behind the driver. Regulations required that a modified have a flat area of no less than 400sq inches behind the cockpit.

MRA Muroc Racing Association

MTA Mojave Timing Association

Overbore An engine with the cylinders enlarged in diameter (bored) to accommodate larger pistons, thus increasing the cubic-inch displacement.

Overhead Term applied to engines with overhead valves, but used most often to describe early Ford flatheads (Model A, B, C, or V-8) with overhead-valve conversions.

Pot Early term for carburettor (see also Jug).

Quick Change Immortalized by Ted Halibrand, the quick change was a specially-made centre section for an early Ford differential banjo housing, which provided two changeable gears behind the ring-and-pinion assembly. By changing these gears, the overall drive ratio could be selected for a particular situation.

Rake Refers to the forward- or rearward-leaning stance of a vehicle, when viewed from the side.

Relieving Removal of the ridge in the top of the block, resulting from counterboring during manufacture for the valve seat.

Reversed Eyes The ends of a standard Ford transverse-leaf spring, curled down and around the shackle pin. When these 'eyes' were reshaped to curl upward, the car was lowered about 1.5 inches, without destroying the spring's effectiveness. In front, though, the clearance in the centre between the spring and axle was reduced.

Ripple Discs The smooth lines of these chrome-plated hubcaps were the 'hot' item for custom rodders in the early 1950s.

RTA Russetta Timing Association, 'russetta' being Greek for 'winged chariot'.

Salt Flats Large expanse of caked salt at the west edge of the Great Salt Lake Desert in Utah, about ten miles east of Wendover.

Tail Job Early streamliner, usually using a sprint car body with a pointed tail.

Tank Short for 'belly tank' or 'drop tank'.

Three-on-the-Tree Column-shift mechanism for a three-speed transmission (the hot-rodders answer to the sporty car set's four-on-the-floor).

Time Hot-rodders sometimes say 'time' when they mean 'speed', because the speed of a race car is calculated from the time it takes to cover a measured distance. So when a rodder says, 'My time was 200mph', he means his time over the distance was equivalent to a speed of 200mph. Through the quarter-mile traps at the dry lakes, his actual time would have been 4.5seconds.

Two-Port Job A Model A or B block with a two-intake-port head (usually applies to a Riley head).

Unlimited Pre-Second World War class for cars with large engines, such as Marmon or Cadillac V16s, or cars with supercharged engines.

V-Butting Hot rod and custom technique of mating two flat windshield sections together at the centre after the centrepost has been removed.

WTA Western Timing Association.

Z'd Frame An effect used to lower a car without affecting suspension geometry. The effect consisted of cutting part of the chassis, raising it and re-welding it to form a 'Z' shape when viewed from the side. This allowed for more clearance for the rear differential or front axle to ride higher in the chassis, thus decreasing the car's overall ground clearance.

This glossary is reproduced by kind permission of **www.rodderboy.com**